Super Chess Kids

Franco Zaninotto

Super Chess Kids

Win Like the World's Young Champions!

New In Chess 2018

Published by New In Chess, Alkmaar, The Netherlands
www.newinchess.com

Cover design: Volken Beck
Supervision: Peter Boel
Editing and typesetting: Frank Erwich
Proofreading: Joe Petrolito
Production: Anton Schermer

Have you found any errors in this book?
Please send your remarks to editors@newinchess.com. We will
collect all relevant corrections on the Errata page of our website
www.newinchess.com and implement them in a possible next edition.

ISBN: 978-90-5691-774-6

Contents

Explanation of symbols

The chessboard
with its coordinates:

±	White stands slightly better
∓	Black stands slightly better
±	White stands better
∓	Black stands better
+−	White has a decisive advantage
−+	Black has a decisive advantage
=	balanced position
!	good move
!!	excellent move
?	bad move
??	blunder
!?	interesting move
?!	dubious move

❑ White to move
■ Black to move
♔ King
♕ Queen
♖ Rook
♗ Bishop
♘ Knight

Preface

Dear reader,

The aim of this book is to improve your understanding of the game
and your practical skills. By reading the book, you'll see that almost
all diagrams are exercises. Please try to answer the question after the
diagram. Active learning is a must if you want to improve.

This book has only junior games (from under 8 to under 14). It has two
parts, namely 'Strategy' and 'Tactics'. Each part has five chapters, three
of which have a theme, some theory and several illustrative games with
exercises. The chapters on strategy (positional play) discuss 'Weaknesses',
'Piece play' and 'Evaluating the position and planning'. Those on tactics
discuss 'Calculation', 'Attack' and 'Defence'. I assume that you have already
an, albeit general, knowledge of strategic and tactical principles. There is a
test at the end of each part with a set of positions to solve.

If you are a junior, I suggest that you look at this book as a challenge. Up
to now, you have probably only looked at games played by masters when
reading other books. Guessing the best move was undoubtedly a bonus
for you. Now, it is different. The games in this book have been played by
juniors in your age group. Guessing the best move now becomes a must.

If you are a chess instructor, this book will help you to identify typical
mistakes made by juniors, and it will give you some tips to correct them. It
also makes available interesting examples to show them.

I trust that the way chess is explained in this book will be easy to
understand. Generally, a good understanding of what weaknesses are
is essential, while good piece play is necessary to exploit weaknesses.
Material, time and space are important if they are useful to create and
exploit weaknesses. Strategy must produce weaknesses in the opponent's
camp, and tactics must exploit them. Hence, everything revolves around
weaknesses.

We may have a good understanding of weaknesses, and still not achieve the desired result! Often we lose not for a lack of knowledge, but because we are unable to use our knowledge. Typical situations are: blundering a piece, not seeing the best move, not seeing a threat, and losing on time. In every situation, there was a weakness (the chess clock is the 33rd piece). We had the knowledge to identify and exploit it, but we didn't do it. Why does this happen? Because we have to improve our way of thinking. This book provides some tools for doing this.

Franco Zaninotto,
Milan, December 2017

PART I

Strategy

CHAPTER 1

Weaknesses

In the middlegame, we need to start an attack. In the past, chess players immediately attacked the opponent's king. Nowadays, this strategy is very difficult to apply, as the openings are played much better. Hence, we usually have to find another way.

The pawn structure might be thought of as the skeleton of a position, and an understanding of it enables us to prepare a good plan. Let's study our opponent's pawn structure (not forgetting that our opponent will do the same with our pawn structure!), and ask ourselves: is it possible now or later to attack some pawns or pieces? Or is it possible to put our pieces on advanced squares where they can't be easily dislodged? This is possible if our opponent's camp has weaknesses. But what is a weakness? A weakness is a square (occupied or not by a piece or a pawn) that can be taken by the opponent. Hence, it is either not defended or not defended sufficiently. Undefended pieces and undefended pawns are therefore weaknesses. A typical weakness is the 'hole'. Steinitz was the first person to use this term in his famous work *The Modern Chess Instructor*. He stated: 'The "hole" means a square on the third or fourth row in front of a pawn after the two adjoining pawns have been moved or captured. Thus, for instance, after the opening moves 1.e4 e5 2.c4, there are already two holes in White's camp, namely, one at d3 and one at d4.

These holes will be all the more dangerous as long as the adverse e-pawn remains at e5, for that pawn stops the advance of two hostile ones [Steinitz means the d- and e-pawns], and by skilful play, Black will retain that advantage for a long time. If White's d-pawn is moved forward to d3, that pawn will be weak, and even if he succeeds in exchanging that pawn for another, the squares at d3 and d4 will remain weak, and White will have to guard against the entrance of hostile men on those squares with one or more pieces, since both the pawns that previously could afford protection against such entrance are advanced.'

Javier Habans Aguerrea   1391
Ciro Revaliente Montoya   1822
Spanish Youth Chess Championship
Salobreña 2016 (U10)

1.e4 c5 2.♘f3 ♘c6 3.♗b5 g6 4.♗xc6 bxc6 5.d3 ♗g7 6.0-0 ♘f6 7.♘c3 0-0 8.♗e3 d6 9.h3 ♖b8 10.♖b1 ♘e8 11.♕d2 f5 12.♗h6?!
12.e5 was better.
12...fxe4 13.♘xe4 ♗xh3! 14.♗xg7

What must Black play? Take the bishop with the king or the knight, or play ...♖xf3?

14...♘xg7??
Black had to defend the 'hole' on h6 with 14...♔xg7!. For example: 15.♕c3+ ♔g8 16.♘eg5 (16.♕d2? ♖xf3!) 16...♗d7 17.♕c4+ ♔g7, and Black remains with an extra pawn. It was not correct to play 14...♖xf3? 15.♗c3! d5 16.♘g3+−.
15.♕h6 ♘f5
After 15...♗f5 16.♘fg5 ♖f6 17.♕xh7+ ♔f8 18.♕h8, Black is mated.
16.♕xh3+−
And White won.

Why did Black make this blunder? It seems that he used only 20 seconds to decide to take with the knight. Too little. He didn't notice that this was a critical position. What is a critical position?

> A position is critical when the position is difficult (mainly tactical), or you have to take a decision that can't be taken back, such as in the case of pawn pushes or exchanges.

It is also possible that Black automatically rejected taking with the king. But the king is not only a strong piece in the endgame, as he can also be very useful in defence. For a king that is under attack, as in this situation, it may be a question of life or death.

In this game, we saw:
1) A bad habit (bad time management);
2) No appreciation or identification of the critical moments;
3) A reluctance to play with the king in the middlegame.

All this is normal, as this was an 'under 10' game. We'll see what to do about the first two points shortly.

Gregoire Brouard   1681
Elliot Papadiamandis   1805
French Junior Chess Championship
Gonfreville 2016 (U12)

1.d4 ♘f6 2.c4 g6 3.♘c3 ♗g7 4.e4 d6 5.♗e2 0-0 6.f4 ♘a6 7.♘f3 e5 8.fxe5 dxe5 9.d5 ♘c5 10.♗d3 ♕e7 11.0-0 ♖e8 12.♗c2 a5 13.h3 ♗d7 14.♗e3 ♘a6 15.a3 ♕d6 16.♕d2 ♖ab8

17.♖f2 b6 18.♖af1 ♖f8 19.♗h6 ♘e8 20.♗xg7

How must Black continue?

Black clearly must take the bishop. If you studied the position carefully, you noted that White has an attack on the king's flank, but without immediate threats. In the previous example, White could successfully attack h7, because Black had pushed and exchanged the f7-pawn. This time, with the f7-pawn on its original square, the same strategy is not fruitful. Hence, it's better not to move the king, which can be more easily attacked. Furthermore, after 20...♔xg7, the ♘e8 remains out of play and prevents the connection between the two rooks.

20...♔xg7?

A mistake. Better was 20...♘xg7 21.♘h2 (after 21.♘b5 ♗xb5 22.cxb5 ♘c5 23.♘g5?! f6, the e6-square is defended by the knight. Better was 23.♕c3 f6±. Attacking, as in the previous example, with 21.♕h6 gives White only a slight plus after 21...f6) 21...f6 22.♘g4 ♘h5, and Black can defend.

21.♘b5!

The game continued with 21.♕g5? f6, with a small advantage to White.

Both 21.♘e2 f6 22.♕c3 and 21.♗a4 ♗xa4 22.♘g5 were interesting.

21...♗xb5

21...♕e7 22.♕c3 f6

analysis diagram

23.♘xe5!, with a great advantage. For example: 23...♘d6 24.♘xd7 ♕xd7 25.♖xf6+−

22.cxb5 ♘c5 23.♘g5 f6 24.b4! axb4 25.axb4 ♘d7 26.♘e6+ ♔g8 27.♘xf8+−

Let's pay great attention to pawn structures, and then we will learn where to put our pieces and how to attack our opponent's pieces.

2016 was a great chess year for the Polish girl Wiktoria Smietanska. In May, she took part in the Polish U8 Chess Championship. For her. it was a training tournament for the U6 Championship, which was to take place later, and Wiktoria was born in 2010. But she surprised everyone and won with 9/9! Afterwards, she took part in the U8 European Union Youth Chess Championship. I suspect that she used it as a training tournament for the European Youth Chess

Championship, and she won in the Girls U8 category!

Afterwards, the European Youth Chess Championship started in Prague. After four rounds, Wiktoria was one of the four girls with a perfect score! Her opponent in the fifth round was the Romanian Maria Lia-Alexandra.

After a tough battle, they arrived at the following position.

Wiktoria Smietanska
Maria Lia-Alexandra   1356

European Youth Chess Championship
Prague 2016 (U8 Girls)

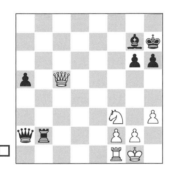

White's position is difficult as Black has a dangerous passed pawn, but it is defendable with correct play.

1) Try to find Black's weaknesses;
2) How would you attack them?

The king is not well-defended. If White removes the ♙g6, the white queen can attack the black king from the f5-h7 diagonal and eventually from the eighth rank (a8-h8). The seventh and eighth rank can be considered, in general, potential weaknesses, as their squares can't be defended by pawns. Usually, they are defended by pieces, but this is not the case

here. Hence, the black king is the weakness that must be attacked.

46.♕c1?

White had to play 46.h4!

A) 46...a4 47.h5 gxh5 48.♕f5+ ♔g8 (48...♔h8?! 49.♖c1 ♖b8 50.♘e5±) 49.♕c8+ ♗f8 (49...♔h7 50.♕f5+=; 49...♔f7?? loses to 50.♖c1, and the rook will reach the seventh rank, as 50...♖b1 loses the rook after 51.♕f5+) 50.♕c6 a3 51.♕g6+ ♗g7 52.♕e8+ ♗f8 53.♕g6+, with perpetual check;

B) 46... ♖b1 47.h5 gxh5 (47...♕e6 48.♖e1 and 47...g5?! 48.♕f5+ ♔g8 49.♕c8+ ♔h7 50.♕d7 a3 51.♖e1 are no better) 48.♕xh5, and now Black must defend, for example with 48...♖b8 49.♖e1 ♖f8 50.♖e7, with a balanced position.

46...a4 47.♕a1

Wiktoria's manoeuvre was clever, but it could only work if Black played 47...♕xa1?. In this case, White would have had realistic drawing chances in the endgame.

47...♕b3 48.♕e1 a3 49.♕e4 a2 50.♘h4 ♕b6 51.♕a4 ♕e6 52.♕a7 ♖b1

And Black won.

> If your opponent has a good pawn structure, see if you can change it into a bad one. This is particularly important if the pawns defend the king.

Wiktoria reacted very well to this defeat, making one and a half point in the following two rounds. Unfortunately, she lost in the last two rounds, although she finished the tournament with a very good 12th place.

What really impressed me about Wiktoria was not her play (although nobody plays the Maroczy Bind against the Accelerated Dragon as well as Wiktoria!), but her time management.

In the FIDE Survey 'Time Trouble', Cuban GM Reinaldo Vera gives this suggestion [quotation slightly modified]: 'To know if you are an unhealthy thinker and what is the moment in the game where you should spend more time, I do recommend you to fill in the following control sheet after each game and after each tournament. If you have time trouble in 4 out of 9 games, or more, obviously you qualify as a thinker.

Games, opponents, ratings.
Time used after 15th move.
Time used after 25th move.
Time used after 35th move.
Moves that took more than 7 minutes.
General evaluation of the time used.

It is important to write down the name of the opponent and his or her Elo, to know if there is a relationship between the strength of the rival and our own time spent.' Vera suggests to use no more than 10 minutes for a move, although other authors have a different opinion. If you generally use more than 7 minutes for a move, you will often get into time trouble. A review of your time usage shows if your time management is good or not.

According to Vera, for a time limit of 90 minutes plus an increment per move for the whole game, the opening moves (the first 15 moves) should generally be made in 15 minutes + the increment. This leaves us with 75 minutes after making our 15th move. From the 16th to the 25th move, we should spend 30 minutes + the increment, so that we have 45 minutes left after the 25th move. This second period of time allows us to handle the transition from the opening to the middlegame, and gives us the time required to develop the typical plans after the opening. From the 26th to the 35th move, we should spend 35 minutes + the increment. After the 35th move, the clock should show 10 minutes. This time control will show if there is a serious time trouble issue.

Let's see how six-year-old Wiktoria and her older opponent managed their time in this game.

Time left after 15th move: Wiktoria 47 minutes, Maria 81 minutes (it must be at least 75 minutes according to Vera);

Time left after 25th move: Wiktoria 17 minutes, Maria 76 minutes (at least 45 minutes according to Vera);

Time left after 35th move: Wiktoria 13 minutes, Maria 68 minutes (at least 10 minutes according to Vera).

Both girls, for different reasons, didn't use their time well. Maria was never in time trouble, but played too quickly. It is a surprise that the younger Wiktoria was the thinker. This was one of Wiktoria's secrets. She often played slowly – too slowly according to Vera's guidelines. However, she made very few mistakes, and she was able to exploit her opponents' poor moves.

> Good time management is very fruitful at junior levels, so it's better to learn this good habit as soon as possible!

After writing down how much time you used during the game, you have to analyse the results. Did you identify and pay enough attention to the critical moments? Look at your mistakes. How much time was dedicated to these moves, and how much time was used for more or less forced moves?

Of course, the help of a chess instructor or an expert player will be very useful to analyse and understand what happened in the game.

Here are some suggestions to avoid time trouble:
• Never be late for a game and arrive a little early to concentrate adequately;
• Decide on the opening you wish to play before the game;
• When there is only one possible move, play it quickly;
• Maintain your concentration, and try to avoid thinking of other things during a game;
• Use your opponent's time mainly for planning.

To improve your time management if you are often in time trouble, play training games and focus primarily on the clock, and not on the quality of the game or the result. Continue this practice until you can manage your time prudently. This approach was suggested by former World Champion Mikhail Botvinnik.

Another good idea is replaying with a friend or a computer the games you lost or were not able to win from the moment of your mistake. This practice will improve your time management, and it will also allow you to practise dealing with difficult positions. Give yourself sufficient time according to the situation. For example, if you made a positional mistake at the 22th move, give yourself 45-50 minutes + increment for the rest of the game.

These suggestions are also applicable for speedy players. There is also another suggestion for these players: 'sit on your hands'.

'The fact that a player is very short of time is, to my mind, as little to be considered an excuse as, for instance, the statement of the law-breaker that he was drunk at the time he committed the crime.' – Alexander Alekhine (former World Champion)

In 2015, the World Youth Championships were held in Halkidiki, Greece. The Indian girl Vaishali Rameshbabu (born in 2001) and her brother Praggnanandhaa Rameshbabu (born in 2005) participated (according to their FIDE profiles, they are simply Vaishali R and Praggnanandhaa R). Previously, Vaishali had won the Under 12 World Championship, and Praggnanandhaa had won the Under 8. In Halkidiki, they won the U14 Girls and U10 Open Championships, respectively. Vaishali was White in the following game.

Rameshbabu Vaishali   2314
Akshaya Kalaiyalahan   2233
World Youth Chess Championship
Halkidiki 2015 (U14 Girls)

How did she improve her position?

25.♘h2!
The knight exploits the hole at g4, and prevents 25...g4.
25...♗d8 26.♘g4 ♘e5?!
Better was 26...♕d6 27.b4!? cxb4 28.axb4 axb4 (28...♘xb4 29.♗a3) 29.♗d2 ♗c7 30.♖fb1, with the initiative. For example: 30...♖h4 31.♗xb4 ♘xb4 32.♗xb7 ♖xg4 (32...♔xb7? 33.♖xb4!) 33.♕f3 ♘d5 34.hxg4 ♔xb7 35.cxd5 exd5 36.♕h3
27.♗xb7 ♘xg4 28.♕xg4 ♕xb7 29.b4!
A very good move. After 29.♕xe6 ♗c7 and 30...♕c8, Black would have some counterplay.
29...axb4 30.axb4 cxb4 31.♗d2 ♕c6 32.♖f7 ♖h4?
A blunder in a very difficult position.
33.♗f4+ ♔c8 34.♕xe6+ 1-0

The Israeli boy Ori Kochavi scored 7 out of 9 and finished 3-10 (9th on tiebreak) at the 2016 U12 European Youth Chess Championship. In the following game, he showed very good positional play.

Ori Kochavi   2038
Ahmad Samir Ahmadzada   2113
European Youth Chess Championship
Prague 2016 (U12 Open)

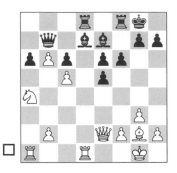

Can White significantly improve his position?
1) **Find Black's weaknesses;**
2) **How would you attack them?**

White takes advantage of the unfortunate position of the black queen.
21.b4!
There is a great hole at a5, and White exploits this weakness.
21...♗c8 22.♘b2!
White improves the position of his worst-placed piece.
22...f5 23.♘c4 e4 24.♘a5
The weak square for Black is a strong square for White.
24...♕a8 25.♖xd8 ♖xd8 26.♖d1
Black is playing without the queen. The game continued with
26...♖e8 27.f3 e5 28.fxe4 f4 29.gxf4 exf4 30.e5 ♗b7 31.♖d7 ♗c8 32.♘xc6 1-0

Pay attention to this manoeuvre. This is a typical way to improve the position of a piece, especially a knight – find a hole and put it there!

A pawn chain consists of at least two pawns placed on the same diagonal without interruption, so that only one of them is undefended. That pawn is called the base of the pawn chain and is a potential weakness.

Nikita Fomin   1591
Gordey Kolesov   1643
World Cadets Chess Championship
Batumi 2016 (U8 Open)

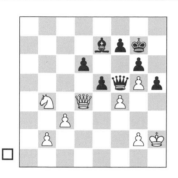

In this example, Black attacked the base of the pawn chain with 49...e5. It seems that only White has weaknesses and that all is lost. But there is a chance. How must White play?
   1) Find Black's weakness;
   2) How would you attack it?

The game continued with
50.fxe5? dxe5 51.♕e3 ♗xg5 52.♕f3 ♕e6 53.♕e2 e4
With a clear advantage for Black. The only move for White was 50.♕e3!. Now, Black can't play 50...exf4, because of 51.♕xe7. The ♗e7 is the weakness that White exploits. The endgame (♘+♙♙♙ against ♗+♙♙♙♙♙) can be saved, thanks to the passed b-pawn. After 50...♕xf4+ (50...♔f8!? 51.♘d5 ♗d8

52.♕h3! ♕e6 53.♕f3=) 51.♕xf4 exf4 52.♘d5 ♗xg5 53.b4 ♗d8 54.b5 g5 55.b6 ♗xb6 56.♘xb6, the endgame is equal. For example: 56...♔f6 57.♔g1 g4 58.♔f2 ♔f5 59.c4 h4 60.♘d5 ♔e5 61.♘c7 ♔d4 62.♘e8 ♔c5 63.♘f6

This was a tough exercise. Many times, we find the right move only because the other possibilities are clearly bad. This forces us to think deeply.

The following game shows how a mechanical move (a move that looks obvious, and so it seems that there is nothing to think about) sometimes can create weaknesses in your own camp.

Matteo Pitzanti   2175
Ilja Semjonovs   2245
World Youth Chess Championship
Khanty-Mansiysk 2016 (U14 Open)

1.d4 ♘f6 2.♘f3 c5 3.e3 cxd4 4.exd4 g6 5.♗f4 ♗g7 6.♗e2 d6 7.0-0 0-0 8.c3 b6 9.♘bd2 ♗b7 10.h3 ♘bd7 11.♖e1 ♕c7 12.♗c4 ♖ae8 13.♕b3 h6 14.♗h2

What should Black play?

14...e5?

This move seems obvious, but it is a mistake in this position. White has a well-posted ♗h2, and after 14...e5, the e5-d6-c7 squares become potentially weak. As the ♗c4 and the ♕b3 form a dangerous battery, Black does better to fight against them by playing 14...♘b8. For example: 15.♖ad1 ♘c6, threatening 16...♘a5. If Black wanted to play ...e7-e5, he had to prepare it with 14...a6, and if 15.a4, then 15...e5.

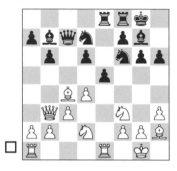

How can White exploit Black's weaknesses?

15.♘h4! d5
The alternative 15...exd4 16.♖xe8 ♘xe8 17.cxd4 ♕d8 18.♘xg6 ♕g5 19.♘f4 ♗xd4 20.♖d1 was a little better, but leaves Black worse anyway.
16.♗b5
Now, it is clear why Black had to play 14...a6. The e5-pawn is very weak and will be lost in a few moves.
16...♖e6 17.♘df3 ♕d8
Now, best was 18.♘xe5 ♘xe5 19.♗xe5, with a clear advantage. The game continued with 18.dxe5?! ♘c5. White eventually won in 31 moves.

Patience and concentration are necessary to avoid such mistakes.

'The word prophylaxis was invented by Aron Nimzowitsch... However, he used it in a very narrow sense. For Nimzowitsch prophylaxis meant prophylactic moves, and this was the prevention of important pawn advances by the opponent. When I started to work on chess, I realized that prophylaxis is much more important in a wider sense – it's a way of thinking. It's a way which helps us to find correct moves. You have to understand what your opponent wants to play. Sometimes you don't need to defend against his ideas. Sometimes you must. So you already have a choice. But the most important thing related to prophylaxis is the skill to ask what your opponent wants to play. If you develop this skill, your play becomes much stronger. Therefore I do not use prophylaxis in my books, but instead use the term "prophylactic thinking". This is because I concentrate on the process of thinking and not the moves. Moves are just the consequences.' – Mark Dvoretsky in his final interview on *Chessbase. com*.

Sometimes, tournaments don't begin very well, but end in glory. This was the case for the Polish girl Alicja Sliwicka at the U14 World Youth Chess Championship in 2015. She began with only two points out of four games, but scored six and a half out of seven in the following games, and she took the silver medal.

Zuzana Gresova 1857
Alicja Sliwicka 2129

World Youth Chess Championship
Halkidiki 2015 (U14 Girls)

Black has just played 16...f4. How would you continue?

17.♕h5?
A mistake. Imagine being White and ask yourself: 'What is my opponent's idea?' The answer is simple: to play 17...f3, creating big problems for White's castled position. Something must be done, and it is clear that White has to prevent this move with 17.♘d2. For example: 17...♚h8 18.♘b4 or 18.♘f3, and while Black can do very little on the king's flank, White has the better prospects on the queen's flank. Perhaps Black could try 17...♗xd5 18.exd5 f3!? 19.♘xf3 ♖f4, but after 20.♖c1 or 20.c5, White would always have a small plus.

Prophylactic thinking is a powerful tool to prevent weaknesses in our position, and it stops our opponent from restricting our pieces. It can sometimes allow us to restrict the mobility of our opponent's pieces.

17...f3! 18.gxf3 ♗xd5 19.exd5

19...♖f4?!
Much stronger was 19...♖f6, threatening 20...♕h3 and 21...♖g6+. For example: 20.♔f1 ♖f4 21.♖e4 ♕h3+ 22.♔e2 g6 23.♖g1 ♗g7–+
20.♖e4 ♖xe4 21.fxe4 ♕h3 22.c5?

White's greatest weakness is her king. How must Black continue the attack?

Black could obtain an immediate decisive advantage with 22...♖f8!! 23.♕e2 (23.cxd6 ♗f4! 24.d7 ♗h2+ 25.♔h1 ♗g3+ 26.♔g1 ♗xf2#) 23...♖f4 24.f3 ♖xf3 and 25...♖g3+. The game continued with 22...♗f4? 23.♕f5, and Black won after some difficulties.

In the following game, we see how we can prevent weaknesses in our position, especially when we are in time trouble.

Czech boy Richard Stalmach played a great European Championship in 2016, scoring 7.5 out of 9 and finishing 1-3 (bronze medal on tiebreak).

Richard Stalmach   1735
Ido Mizrahi   1827
European Youth Chess Championship
Prague 2016 (U10 Open)

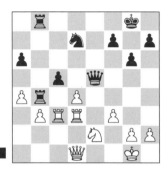

Black had to give a pawn (28...d4 29.exd4), but the activity of Black's rooks is not enough to compensate for this. Anyway, many pieces are in play and everything can happen. At this point, Black had only four minutes left, and used three of these on the next move.

29...cxd4?

I doubt that Black thought of his opponent's threats before playing this move. Probably, he thought about the activity of his pieces. Black had to play 29...♕e7. After 30.♕d2 cxd4 (30...a5!?) 31.♖xd4 (31.♘xd4?! ♘e5 32.♖e3 ♕d6 33.♖xe5 ♖xd4 34.♕e3 ♖d1+ 35.♔f2 ♖d2+ 36.♔f1=) 31...♘c5, Black has some pressure against b3.

30.♘xd4

Now, Black cannot prevent the fork.

30...♘c5?!

Giving up the exchange with 30...♖xd4 was a little better, although Black still has a lost position.

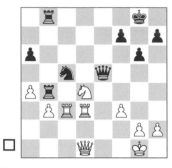

31.♘c6

The fork! Black did not notice a very weak square in his camp, and the knight is extremely happy to exploit it!

31...♕c7 32.♘xb4 ♖xb4 33.♖d5 ♖h4 34.♖cxc5 ♕xh2+ 35.♔f2

And Black resigned.

Black had to make a blunder check before taking the pawn. In other words, imagine yourself playing the move and thinking: 'Does it blunder something?'

A common way to lose a game is to make a blunder. Hence, it is better to make a quick blunder check before playing critical moves, especially with little time (but not in terrible time trouble!).

What can you do to learn this skill? Try to play with a training partner, and try making a blunder check before every move. It will take some time, but gradually blunder checking will be internalized and done when needed.

Blunder checking is a powerful tool to prevent weaknesses and blunders. Another tool to avoid mistakes is the 'sense of danger'. To improve this, pay attention to the links between pieces, namely which pieces are protecting other pieces. Be aware if something in the position changes.

Iranian girl Hasti Khosravi Mahmoei won bronze at the World Cadets Chess Championship (U8 Girls) 2016.

Hasti Khosravi Mahmoei   1254
Deniza Kurmanalina

World Cadets Chess Championship
Batumi 2016 (U8 Girls)

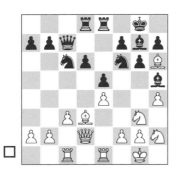

Black has a very badly-placed ♗h5. Can White exploit this situation and create new weaknesses in Black's position?

18.♗g5!
Now, Black can't prevent the weakening of her king's flank. The game continued with 18.♕g5?! ♘e7, and White was only a little better.
18...♖d7 19.♗xf6 ♗xf6 20.♘xh5 gxh5 21.g3 ♕b6 22.♕e2 ♗g7 23.♖c2 ♖e6 24.♕xh5+–

Lance Henderson de la Fuente   2180
Filip Haring   2107

World Youth Chess Championship
Halkidiki 2015 (U12 Open)

1.e4 c5 2.♘f3 e6 3.b3 ♘f6 4.e5 ♘d5 5.♗b2 ♘c6 6.g3 ♗e7 7.♗g2 0-0 8.0-0 f6 9.♘a3 d6 10.exf6 ♘xf6 11.d4 d5 12.c4 cxd4 13.cxd5 exd5 14.♘c2 ♗g4 15.♘cxd4 ♕d7

It's clear that White is better, with Black having an isolated pawn. But how does White continue?

When there is a possibility of reaching an endgame, we must evaluate the new situation. Is this better than keeping all the pieces on the board? We have to answer the question: will Black's weaknesses be greater than now or not?
16.♘xc6!
Better than 16.♖c1 ♗d6 17.♘xc6 (17. h3 ♗xh3 18.♗xh3 ♕xh3 19.♘xc6 bxc6 20.♖xc6 ♕d7±) 17...bxc6 18.♕c2 ♖ac8±.
16...bxc6
Or 16...♕xc6 17.♘e5 ♗xd1 18.♘xc6 bxc6 19.♖fxd1, with an endgame similar to the game.
17.♘e5 ♗xd1 18.♘xd7 ♘xd7 19.♖fxd1

19...♗f6?!

Better is 19...♗c5 20.♖d2 ♖ae8 21.♖c1, with a difficult position for Black, but with chances to hold.

analysis diagram

For example: 21...♖f7 22.♗h3 ♗b4 23.♖dc2 ♘b8 24.f4 ♗d6 25.♗g4, and White will torture Black for a long time.

20.♗xf6 ♘xf6 21.♖ac1 ♖ac8 22.♗h3 ♖ce8 23.♖xc6 ♖e2 24.a4 ♘e4 25.♖c8 ♖xc8 26.♗xc8 ♘xf2 27.♖xd5
And White won the endgame.

Before concluding this chapter, I want to underline that weaknesses have many causes and can be exploited in different ways. The better you know these ways, the better you will play chess.

It is very important to have a good understanding of our openings. If you know their pawn structures well, you know where weaknesses can rise, and where the pieces are better – or poorly – placed. Pay attention to the typical tactical blows that can provoke weaknesses (for example, ...♖xc3 in the Sicilian). Pay attention to typical piece manoeuvres that can provoke or prevent weaknesses (for example, how to exchange a fianchettoed bishop and how to avoid the exchange). You need a simple reference point when you play, and so look for weaknesses!

CHAPTER 2

Piece play

In the first chapter, we discussed primarily squares and pawns. In this chapter, there will be much more about space for pieces. Summarizing:

1) We have to place our pieces in active and strong positions;
2) We have to prevent our opponent from doing the same. In other words, we have to restrict the mobility of our opponent's pieces.

Vladislav Kochetov   1703
Egor Sokolov   1247
European Youth Chess Championship
Porec 2015 (U8 Open)

White has a difficult position. How can he improve it?

I suppose that before playing
27.♘c2!
the very young Vladislav remembered what every coach tells pupils, namely the famous Tarrasch quote: 'If one piece is badly-placed, your game is bad.' Hence, he looked for a better square for his ♘a3.
27...♕h6 28.♘e3 ♖3d6
The computer suggests 28...♗xh3. Probably, this was the best move, but when you have a positional advantage, it is not logical to enter into a complicated and unsure variation: 29.gxh3 ♕xh3+ 30.♔g1

♘g5, and now for example: 31.♘ef1 ♕h6 32.♗c2 ♖3d4 33.♘b3 ♖xd1 34.♖xd1 ♘h3+ 35.♔h1 ♘f2+ 36.♔g2 ♘xd1 37.♗xd1, and although Black seems better, nothing is clear.
29.♘d5

White has improved his position and the play is now more or less equal. This can be a little annoying for Black. How should he continue?

29...♗xd5?
A mistake. A good idea would have been to attack the white weaknesses on h3 and d4 with 29...♘g5!, putting pressure on h3 and preparing ...♗d7 and ...♘e6-d4.
30.cxd5
Now, two of White's badly-placed pieces find a new life. The ♘d2 will have a good square on c4 and the ♗b3 returns to serve as a bishop (before, it served as a pawn).

Before exchanging, you should focus on which pieces remain on the board, rather than on the ones you exchange.

After 30...♖6d7 (the game continued with 30...♕f4?!, and White could take advantage of this by playing 31.♘c4, for example: 31...♖6d7 32.b6! axb6 33.♘xb6! ♖7d6 34.♘a4 ♖6d7?! 35.d6+–) 31.b6! axb6 (31...a6? 32.♗a4! ♖e7 33.♘c4, with ideas such as 34.d6 and 34.♕f2) 32.axb6 ♘d6 33.♖c1, White has a clearly better game.

Pay attention to your worst-placed pieces and look for and eventually create better squares for them. If it is not possible to create such squares, try to press your opponent and perhaps he will do it for you!

Piece play is often tied with little tactical tricks that can lead to positional or material advantages.

Alejandro Valenzuela Fernandez 1483
Alfonso Gutierrez Guillen 1301
Spanish Youth Championship
Salobreña 2016 (U10)

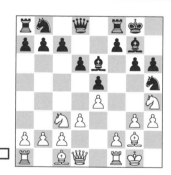

What is your move with white?

Now, White played 10.♘e2. It was much better to exploit the bad ♘h5 position with
10.♘f5! ♔h7
10...gxf5 11.exf5 (11.♕xh5 f4 12.gxf4 exf4 13.♘e2! ♘c6 14.♘xf4+–) ♗xf5 12.♗xb7+–
11.♘xg7 ♔xg7
A little better than 11...♘xg7 12.♕d2 g5 (12...♖h8 13.f4!) 13.f4!.
12.d4
White has the bishop pair and much more play.

Martin Stukan 1962
Andrei Ioan Trifan 2069
European Youth Chess Championship
Prague 2016 (U12 Open)

Is ♙a2 poisoned?

20...♗xa2!
White keeps an advantage after 20...♗c5+ 21.♔h1. For example: 21...♕e5 22.a4 ♗c6 23.axb5 axb5 24.♗b3 ♗d6 25.♕g1
21.b3?
Better is a normal developing move like 21.♗e3. After 21...♖d8 22.♕e2 ♗c4 23.♕f2 f6 24.g3 (24.♖xa6? ♗xh2+) 24...b4 25.cxb4 ♗xb4, the game is nearly equal.
21...♖d8!

24

A clever trick to attack the white queen, one of the defenders of the ♗b3.

22.♗d2

22.♔h1 ♗e7 23.♗d2 ♗g5 24.♖xa2 ♖xd2 25.♕f1 g6, with advantage to Black.

22...♗f4 23.♗xf4 ♖xd1+ 24.♖xd1 h5

It was a little better to play 24...h6 25.♖d8+ ♔h7 26.♖d5 ♕b6+ 27.♔f1 a5, with a clear advantage to Black.

25.♖d8+ ♔h7 26.♗g5?

26.♖d5 ♕c6 27.♗d2 a5

26...♗xb3

And Black won.

Kaiyu Ning 2066
Yili Wen 1726

World Cadets Chess Championship

Batumi 2016 (U12 Girls)

What is your move with black?

In this position, Black has a very weak d6-pawn, but White has some weaknesses, too.

21...♘c5!

The game continued with 21...♖e6?! 22.♖gd1 ♘e5?! (better was 22...♕a5 23.♕e1) 23.♖xb4, with advantage to White.

22.♘xc5

Or 22.♕c4 ♖xe4 23.♖gd1 ♕c6 24.♗xd6 ♖xd4 25.♖xd4 ♘e6

26.♕xc6 ♗xc6 27.♖xb4 ♘xg5. Of course, not 22.♗xd6?? ♘xb3+ 23.♔b1 ♘xd4.

22...♕xc5 23.♖gd1 ♖ae8

With counterplay. For example: 24.♕d2 (24.♗xd6 ♕xg5+=) 24...♖xe4 25.♗xd6 ♕a5 26.♔b1 ♖xd4 27.♕xd4 ♕xg5 28.♖g1 ♖e4 29.♕a7 ♕b5 30.♗xb4 ♕xb4 31.♕b8+ ♕f8 32.♕xb7 ♖e6 33.h4 ♕e8, with an even game.

Rameshbabu Vaishali 2124
Teodora Rogozenco 1974

World Youth Chess Championship

Durban 2014 (U14 Girls)

White has the initiative. How must Black defend?

Black is behind in development and must coordinate her pieces. The worst placed piece is the ♘h6, and so the best move is

16...♗f7!

16...♗g8 was not the same: 17.♗xg8 ♖xg8 18.♘c4, with the threat 19.♖xd7, and White is better. For example: 18...axb4! 19.♖hd1 bxa3 20.♖xd7 ♗c5 21.♘fxe5 a2 22.♔b2 a1♕+ 23.♖xa1 ♖xa1 24.♔xa1 fxe5 25.♘xe5, and White is a pawn up. Worse is 18...b5? 19.♖hd1 bxc4 20.♖xd7, and Black, not having 20...♘d6, is lost. The game continued with 16...♗xc4? 17.♘xc4 b5 18.♖hd1 bxc4 19.♖xd7 ♖b8, and now best was 20.♘xe5 fxe5 21.♖a7+−.

17.♗xf7

17.♖hd1 ♘b6 18.♖d8+ ♔c7=

17...♘xf7

Now, White's weaknesses (especially b4 and e4) will be attacked by Black's pieces. Pay attention to the badly-placed ♘f3 and ♗h4.

18.♘c4 b5 19.♘xa5

19.♖hd1 bxc4 20.♖xd7 ♘d6! 21.♖1xd6 ♗xd6 22.♖xg7 (22.♖xd6?! ♔c7 23.♖d1 axb4−+) 22...axb4 23.axb4 c3∓

19...♖xa5 20.bxa5 ♗xa3+ 21.♔d1 ♘c5 22.♖e2 ♘d6 23.c3 ♘dxe4

With a slight advantage for Black.

Yuliya Vinokur   1976
Grete Olde   1727
European Youth Chess Championship
Prague 2016 (U14 Girls)

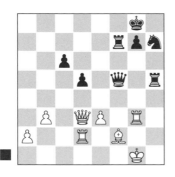

The previous move was 45.♕d3. How must Black continue?

45...♘g5?

As Black's queen is an active and dangerous piece, Yuliya offered the queen exchange, and surprisingly, Grete didn't avoid it! Black had

to play 45...♕f6 (45...♕e6 is not as good), and not exchange the queens or permit this exchange. After 45...♕f6, Black has a great advantage, for example: 46.♕d4 ♕h6 47.♔f1 ♘g5−+ or 46.♖g6 ♕f3 47.♔f1 ♘g5−+.

46.♕xf5 ♖xf5 47.♖c2 ♘h3+?!

Black again wants to exchange pieces, while 47...♘e4 48.♖g4 c5 gave her a slightly better position.

48.♔g2 ♘xf2 49.♖xf2 ♖h2+ 50.♔xh2 ♖xf2+ 51.♖g2 ♖f3 52.♖e2 ♔f7 53.♔g2 ♖f6 54.b4 ♔e6

With a level endgame that Black eventually won.

> It is always useful to exchange the opponent's strongest pieces. This is more evident when under attack, but it is also helpful in quiet positions.

The following game is very interesting for examining weaknesses and the coordination of the pieces.

Danitza Vazquez Maccarini   1935
Shengxin Zhao   1766
World Youth Chess Championship
Durban 2014 (U14 Girls)

1.e4 c5 2.♘f3 ♘c6 3.♗b5 g6 4.♗xc6 dxc6 5.d3 ♕c7 6.♗e3 ♗g7 7.♘c3 b6 8.h3 e5 9.♕d2 ♘e7 10.♗h6 0-0 11.h4 f6 12.♗xg7 ♔xg7 13.h5 g5 14.♕e3 h6 15.♘e2 ♗g4 16.♘g3 ♖ad8 17.♘h2 ♗e6 18.b3 ♘c8 19.♕f3 ♕d7 20.0-0 ♘d6 21.a4 a5 22.♖fe1 ♘c8 23.♕d1 ♖f7 24.♘gf1 ♔h7 25.g4 ♘d6 26.♘e3 ♘b7 27.♘c4 ♕c7 28.♕f3 b5 29.axb5 cxb5 30.♘e3 ♕d7

Puerto Rican Danitza Vazquez Maccarini and Chinese Shengxin Zhao were in zeitnot (a couple of minutes for each of them) when, after a well-played positional battle, they reached the position in the following diagram.

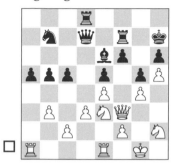

How should White continue?

White could improve her worst-placed piece with 31.♘hf1!, preparing a jump to g3 or eventually to e3. For example: 31...a4 (31...♖a8 32.♘d5 ♕d8 33.♘fe3) 32.bxa4 bxa4 33.♖a3 ♖a8 34.♖ea1 ♘d6 35.c4 ♕e8 36.♘g3 In the game, White went for a tactical trick.

31.♘d5 ♗xd5 32.exd5

To take or not to take? That's the question.

It was correct to take the pawn with 32...♕xd5!. Black feared 33.♕f5+ ♔h8 34.♕g6, but after 34...♕e6

35.♕xh6+ ♖h7 36.♕g6 ♘d6!, White's queen risks being trapped. She can escape with 37.d4, but Black is better after 37...cxd4 38.♖xa5 e4 39.♖ea1 ♖g7 40.♕h6+ ♔g8 41.♖a8 ♖xa8 42.♖xa8+ ♘c8. Hence, 31.♘d5 was a doubtful move. When you have little time left, it is usually better to avoid tactical variations.

Piece coordination is a very important principle in chess, but it is difficult to explain in a useful way. Usually, it is the action of a player's pieces when they work together, or the 'teamwork' of the pieces. But with what scope? I'll give another definition.

Piece coordination is the use of two or more pieces to jointly exploit or cover one or more weaknesses. For example, if the weakness to exploit is only one square, the pieces concentrate on it, or on it and its defenders. A typical way to do this is to eliminate the defenders. Imagine a position where Black has the weak square d5 defended only by the ♘f6. White exploits this by playing ♗g5 and ♗xf6, permitting the ♘c3 to go to d5. If there are several weak squares – in the game we just examined, these squares were those where the white queen could go – the pieces have to cover all of them by sharing the work. If we find a weakness and decide that two or more of our pieces must act, let's always find the most effective way in which they can work together.

In the game, play continued with
32...Re8 33.c4 b4

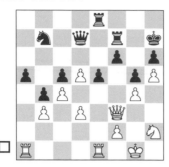

How should White continue?

There are two good ideas, namely the standard 34.♘f1 and 34.♕e4+:

A) 34.♘f1 f5 35.♘g3 e4 (35...fxg4? 36.♕e4+ ♔h8 37.♕g6+−) 36.dxe4 fxe4 37.♕g2 ♕xg4 38.♘xe4 ♕d7 39.♖e3 ♖ef8 40.♖a2;

B) 34.♕e4+ f5 (34...♔h8 35.♕g6 ♕e7 36.♕xh6+ ♖h7 37.♕g6 ♘d6 38.d4 cxd4 39.♖xa5) 35.♕g2, provoking new weaknesses: 35...♕c7 36.gxf5 ♖xf5 37.♘g4 ♕f7 38.♖e3

In both cases, White is better.

The game continued with
34.♕g3 f5 35.♖xe5?? f4 36.♕g2 ♖xe5 37.♘f3 ♖e8 38.d4 ♖fe7 39.♘e5 ♘d6?? 40.♘xd7 1-0

Anastasiia Dubovyk	1785
Isil Can	1945

European Youth Chess Championship
Mamaia 2017 (U12 Girls)

1.e4 e5 2.♘f3 ♘c6 3.♗b5 a6 4.♗a4 ♘f6 5.0-0 ♗e7 6.♖e1 b5 7.♗b3 d6 8.c3 0-0 9.h3 ♘a5 10.♗c2 c5 11.d4 ♕c7 12.♘bd2 cxd4 13.cxd4 ♗d7 14.♘f1 ♖ac8 15.♗b1 ♘c6 16.♗e3 a5 17.♗d3 ♕b7 18.a3 ♗d8 19.d5 ♘e7 20.♘g3 ♘g6 21.♕d2 ♗b6 22.♗g5 ♘e8 23.h4 f6 24.♗e3 ♗xe3 25.♕xe3 ♘f4

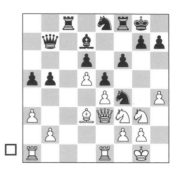

Must White try to exchange Black's ♘f4 with 26.♘e2 or play something else?

26.♘e2?!
With this move, White accelerates Black's attack. Better was 26.♗f1 ♖c2?! (26...g6 27.h5 f5 28.hxg6 hxg6 29.exf5 gxf5 30.♘e2 ♘xd5 31.♕h6 is unclear) 27.♖ac1 ♕c7 (27...♖xb2? 28.♕c3 ♖a2 29.♕b3) 28.♖ed1± or 26.♖ac1, with mutual chances.

26...♘xd3 27.♕xd3 f5! 28.♘g3!
28.♘g5 h6 29.♘e6 fxe4 30.♕d2 ♖f6∓

28...f4 29.♘f1 ♘f6 30.♖ac1 ♖xc1 31.♖xc1 ♖c8 32.♖c2 b4 33.axb4 axb4 34.♘3d2 ♖xc2 35.♕xc2

Black is slightly better, but what should she play now?

35...♕c8?!
After the exchange of the queens, the b4-pawn will be weaker, and the play will be more or less even.

Black should improve her position on the kingside. For example: 35...h6 36.♕c4 ♕b6 37.b3 ♔h7, with the ideas of ...g7-g5 and ...♘g4.
36.♕xc8+ ♗xc8 37.f3 ♗a6 38.♘b3 ♘d7 39.♘fd2 ♔f7 40.♘a5 ♘c5 41.♘dc4 ♔e7 42.♘c6+ ♔d7 43.♘d2 ♗b5 44.♘xb4 ♘d3 45.♘xd3 ♗xd3 46.♔f2 h6 47.g3 g5 48.hxg5 hxg5 49.gxf4 gxf4 50.♔g2 ♔c7 51.♔h3 ♔b6 52.♔g4 ♔c5 53.♘b3+

We have reached an interesting endgame. Only one move saves Black. Which one?

53...♔b4?

A) 53...♔b6? is not sufficient: 54.♔f5 ♗e2 55.♘d2 ♔c7 56.♔e6 ♗d3 57.♔e7 ♗e2 58.♔e6 ♗b5 59.b3 ♗d3 60.♘c4 ♗e2 61.♘xd6 ♗xf3 62.♔e7 ♗g4 63.♘f5+−;

B) Black had to activate her king with 53...♔c4!. For example: 54.♘d2+ (54.♘a5+ ♔d4 55.♘c6+ ♔e3 56.♘e7 ♔xe4 57.fxe4 f3 58.♘f5+ ♔xe4 59.♘xd6+ ♔xd5 60.♘f5 ♔c4 61.♔xf3 ♔b3=; after 54.♘c1? ♗f1 55.♔f5 ♗h3+ 56.♔f6 ♗g2, White can't play 57.♘d3 as in the game and is worse) 54...♔d4 (54...♔c5!? 55.♔f5 ♔d4 56.♔e6 ♔e3 is another drawing line) 55.b3 ♗e2 56.♘c4 ♔c5 57.♘a5 ♔b6 58.♘c6 ♔c7 59.♘e7 ♗d1 60.b4 ♗e2 61.♘g6 ♔d7

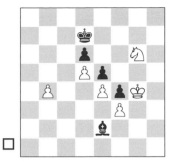

analysis diagram

As it seems that White cannot obtain anything by manoeuvring, the last try could be to sacrifice the knight for two pawns: 62.♘xf4 exf4 63.♔xf4 ♗f1 64.♔e3 ♗a6 65.f4 ♔e7 66.e5 ♗b5 67.♔d4 ♗f1 68.f5 dxe5+ 69.♔xe5 ♗b5 70.d6+ ♔f7! (70...♔d7 71.f6 ♗c4 72.♔d4 ♗f7 73.♔c5 ♗g6 74.b5 ♔d8 75.b6 ♔c8 76.♔b5 ♗d3+ 77.♔b4 ♗g6 78.♔a5 ♗f7 79.♔a6+−) 71.♔d5 ♗d7=
54.♘c1 ♗f1 55.♔f5 ♗h3+
55...♗g2 56.♘d3+ ♔b5 57.♘e1 ♗h3+ 58.♔f6 ♔b6 59.♔e7 ♔c7 60.♘d3 ♗d7 61.♘b4 ♗c8 62.♘c6 ♗d7 63.♘d8 ♗g4 64.♘e6+ ♔b6 65.♘g5 ♗c8 66.♔xd6+−
56.♔f6 ♗g2
56...♔c5 57.♘e7 ♗g2 58.b4+ ♔xb4 59.♔xd6 ♗xf3 60.♔xe5+−
57.♘d3+ ♔b3 58.♘e1 ♗h3 59.♔e7 ♔xb2 60.♔xd6 ♔c3 61.♔xe5 ♔d2 62.♔xf4 ♔xe1 63.♔e3 ♔d1 64.f4 ♔c2 65.f5 ♗g4 66.d6 ♔c1 1-0

The following game, played at the World Youth Chess Championship (U10 Girls) 2015, between Azeri Ayan Allahverdiyeva and the then under 10 World Champion (Durban 2014), Indian Deshmukh Divya, was a very interesting fight.

Ayan Allahverdiyeva   1657
Deshmukh Divya   1772
World Youth Chess Championship
Halkidiki 2015 (U10 Girls)

**1.e4 c5 2.c3 g6 3.d4 cxd4 4.cxd4 d5
5.e5 ♗g7 6.♘c3 ♘c6 7.♗e3 ♘h6
8.♘f3 ♗g4 9.h3 ♗xf3 10.♕xf3 e6?!**

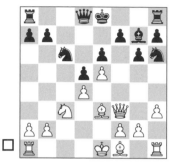

Find White's best move.

After 11.0-0-0 ♘f5 12.g4 ♘xe3
13.♕xe3 ♖c8 or 11.♗d3 0-0 12.0-0
f6 13.exf6 ♖xf6, Black would have
at least a level game. Hence, White
played

11.g4!

White prevents ...♘f5, and Black's
knight is out of play at the moment.
For this reason, Black had to play
10...♘f5!, with a good game.

11...0-0

**An important moment in the
game. How must White play?**

**Remember 'weaknesses' and
'improving your worst-placed
piece'.**

12.♕d1?!

Ayan played this after thinking
for nearly one minute. 12.♕e2,
with the same idea (13.♕d2), but
permitting castling, was better.
For example: 12...♕h4 13.0-0-0 f6
14.f4 fxe5 15.fxe5 ♘f7 16.♔b1, with
better play for White, who can
play on both flanks. For example:
16...♖ac8 17.♗f2!? ♕e7 18.h4
If 12...♔h8, 13.♕d2, and we return
to the game.

12...♔h8?!

Too passive. Black had to play
12...♕h4, with more or less an equal
game after 13.♗e2 (or 13.♕d2 ♘xg4
14.♗g5 ♕h5! 15.♗e2 ♘xd4 16.♕xd4
♕xg5 17.hxg4 ♗xe5) 13...f6 14.exf6
♗xf6 15.♕d2 ♘f7 16.0-0-0 ♖ae8.

13.♕d2 ♘g8

How must White continue?

14.h4?!

White had to play 14.0-0-0, and if
14...f6, then 15.f4. For example: 15...
fxe5 16.fxe5 ♕h4 17.♔b1 a6 18.♘a4 If
Black doesn't play 14...f6, it doesn't
make sense to play 15.f4, losing a
tempo and closing the diagonal to
the ♗e3. Hence, after for example

14...♘ge7, then 15.h4, and if 14...♕h4, then 15.♔b1 h6 16.♘b5.

Black's main weakness is the position of the king. Ayan understood this immediately and chose the best plan (the attack on the rook file), but applied it incorrectly.

14...f6 15.f4 fxe5 16.fxe5

How must Black continue?

16...♗xe5!

Best. An attack on the flank needs a stable centre (Steinitz). This is not the case, and Deshmukh exploits this. After 16...♖c8 17.0-0-0 or 16...♕b6 17.h5 g5 18.0-0-0, White could quietly continue her attack.

17.dxe5 d4 18.0-0-0 dxe3 19.♕xe3 ♕a5

Better is 19...♕b6 20.♕xb6 axb6 21.g5 ♘ge7 22.♗c4 ♘xe5 23.♗xe6, with only a small plus for White.

20.h5

Better is 20.♗b5 ♘b4 21.a4.

20...♕xe5 21.♕xe5+ ♘xe5 22.hxg6 ♘xg6 23.♖d7

With a slight advantage for White, who eventually won.

The Indian girl recovered well from this defeat and by winning the last three games of the tournament she took bronze, while the Azeri girl finished sixth.

Artur Avalyan 2277
Eelke De Boer 2233
European Youth Chess Championship
Mamaia 2017 (U14 Open)

What should White play?

26.♔e2?!

White had 26.b6! ♘xb6 27.♘c5, with full compensation for the pawn. For example: 27...♖e8 28.♘e6 ♕b8 29.h4 g4 30.g3 a5 31.gxf4, with a complicated position where White seems better. Indeed, the exercise has a second, more positional solution, which I'll give you only after the next exercise.

What should Black play?

26...♕b8!

Black exchanges his bad bishop, solving all his problems. White could prevent this by playing 26.♘b2!? (the second solution)

26...♕b8 27.♘c4 ♗b6 28.♘xb6 axb6. In this case, the game would have been nearly equal.

27.g3

27.g4 ♘f7 28.h4 ♗b6 29.hxg5 ♕d8∓

27...♗b6 28.h4?!

28.♗xb6 axb6∓

28...g4 29.gxf4 exf4

And after

30.fxg4?!

(30.♗xb6 axb6 31.♘xf4 gxf3+ 32.♔xf3 ♖xa1 33.♖xa1 ♕e8∓)

30...♕e8!

Black is clearly better. The game continued with 30...♘xg4?!, and finished with a draw after nearly thirty more moves.

Let's now see an exemplary game about weaknesses. We'll see, moreover, that it pays to study the methods of handling pawn structures that aren't supposed to arise from our openings. Romanian boy Mihnea-Jonut Ognean played the following game (a good example of positional play) in the ninth and final round of the 2015 European Union Youth Chess Championship (U12 Open). Before the game, four players were 1st-4th, and Ognean and the Armenian boy Mamikon Gharibyan were two of them.

Mihnea-Jonut Ognean	2164
Mamikon Gharibyan	2106

European Youth Chess Championship
Porec 2015 (U12 Open)

1.e4 c5 2.c3 d6 3.d4 ♘f6 4.♗d3 ♘c6 5.♘f3 e5 6.dxe5 dxe5 7.0-0 ♗e7 8.♕e2 0-0 9.a4 h6 10.♘a3 ♕c7

11.♘c4 ♗e6 12.b3 a6 13.♕c2 ♖fd8 14.♖d1 ♖ab8 15.♘e3

What should Black play?

White has lost some tempi with the queen and the knight, and Black now had the chance to play 15...b5, with a good position. Instead, he preferred to create two holes in White's camp, namely on b4 and d4. However, White will take more advantages: a strong outpost on d5, an open diagonal for the ♗c1 and two tempi.

15...♘a5?! 16.c4 ♘c6 17.♘d5

What should Black play?

17...♗xd5?

As we saw previously, exchanging is often a critical move. In this case, it was correct to exchange, but only to have the chance to put the knight on d4. For example: 17...♕d7 18.h3 ♗xd5 19.cxd5 ♘d4 20.♘xd4 cxd4,

with nearly an even game. Note that
Black loses an important bishop,
but gives some air to the ♗e7 by
playing 20...cxd4.

18.cxd5 ♘b4

Not 18...♘d4?! 19.♘xd4 exd4 (19...
cxd4?? 20.♕xc7) 20.f4, with a clearly
better game for White.

19.♕e2 ♘xd3 20.♕xd3

Now, Black had to go for
counterplay on the queen's flank
with 20...b5. After 21.axb5 axb5
22.♗b2 c4 23.bxc4 bxc4, White
would have had only a small plus.

**20...♗d6?! 21.♘h4 ♗f8 22.♘f5 ♔h7
23.♗b2 g6 24.♘e3**

24...♗d6

Black prepares an attack on the
king's flank, but by doing so he
leaves the queen's flank to White. It
was better to play 24...b5.

**25.♘c4 ♘d7 26.a5 ♖f8 27.f3 ♖be8
28.♖f1 f5 29.g3**

Not necessary. Better was 29.♖fe1.

29...f4

White has active pieces and a better
pawn structure. It's clear that
Black made a mistake by playing
17...♗xd5, and that afterwards he
chose a wrong plan by trying to
attack on the king's flank. The game
is similar to a King's Indian, but
Black doesn't have the light-squared
bishop, which is a very important
attacking piece in that opening
with the king's flank closed. Hence,
White can close it and focus his
attention on the queen's flank.

> Some pawn structures may be
> good for one side, providing that a
> particular type of piece is present.

30.g4!?

Not the only move, but a good one.

30...♖b8

  A) Not 30...h5?! 31.gxh5 gxh5
32.♔h1 ♖g8 33.♖g1, with the idea
34.♖xg8 ♖xg8 35.♕f1 and 36.♕h3;

  B) There are no chances to
attack on the king's flank, so Black
changed his plan and brought his
pieces to the other flank. It was
probably better to improve the
position of the queen, which is not
stable on c7, with 30...♘f6, 31...♕e7
and eventually ...♘d7.

31.♖fc1

White's weaknesses – b4 and d4 – can't be exploited, because by taking on d5, Black gave White an outpost that prevents Black's knight jumps.

31...♖fc8 32.♗c3 ♖a8 33.♔h1 ♕b8 34.♗e1 ♔g7 35.♕e2 ♔f7 36.♕b2

36...b5
Other moves are not better:
36...♗f8 37.♗c3 ♔g7 38.b4 or 36...♔f8 37.b4.

37.axb6 ♘xb6 38.♘a5 ♘d7 39.♗c3 ♖e8 40.♕e2 ♔f6 41.♖cb1 ♗c7 42.♘c4 ♕b5 43.♕d2 ♘b6?
A blunder in a lost position (43...g5 44.d6 ♗d8 45.♕b2+−).

44.♕xf4+ ♔g7 45.♘xe5
And White won.

Ognean finished 1st-2nd, taking the silver medal on tiebreak.

CHAPTER 3

Evaluating the position and planning

A plan in chess is a set of actions that have been thought of as a way to achieve something. Mating the enemy king would be the best result, but usually we must moderate our goal. As Steinitz showed, the plan must be realistic. Before planning, we must correctly evaluate the position. Steinitz described many elements of planning. I want to give you, very briefly, three more recent approaches.

In his book *Think like a Grandmaster*, Alekander Kotov identified four major categories of positional elements that are useful for evaluating a position (assuming material is equal). By comparing these elements, the chess player makes an evaluation of the position, sets a goal and prepares a plan.

1) Open lines and diagonals;
2) Pawn structure and weak squares;
3) Piece position;
4) Space and the centre.

In their book *Find the Plan*, Karpov and Matsukevich quote seven principles or reference points, according to which the study of any position should be undertaken:

1) Material relationship between the forces;
2) Presence of direct threats;
3) Positions of the kings, their safety;
4) Possession of open lines;
5) Pawn structure, weak and strong squares;
6) The centre and space;
7) Development and the position of pieces.

According to the authors, 'restricting the mobility of your opponent's pieces (and in association with this: domination by your own) is the most important law in chess.' Mate is an attack to a chess monarch whose movement is completely restricted.

In his book *How to Reassess Your Chess*, Jeremy Silman uses the term 'imbalance'. An imbalance denotes any difference in the two respective positions. The real goal of a chess game is to create an imbalance and try to build a situation in which it is favourable for you. There are seven kinds of imbalances:

1) Superior minor piece (the interplay between bishops and knights);
2) Pawn structure (a broad subject that encompasses doubled pawns, isolated pawns, etc.);
3) Space (the annexation of territory on the chess board);
4) Material (owning pieces of greater value than the opponent's);
5) Control of a key file or square (files and diagonals act as pathways for your pieces, while squares act as homes);
6) Lead in development (more force in a specific area of the board);
7) Initiative (dictating the tempo of a game).

I assume that you have some knowledge, albeit general, of the points quoted in these books. The better you know them, the more easily you'll identify the best plan. This is because, for finding the best plan, we must correctly evaluate the consequences both of our options and those of our opponent (prophylactic thinking teaches us that an optimal plan always has to take into account the opponent's options). To achieve this, we must know, for example, that with a particular pawn structure, certain pieces should be exchanged and others not, a certain kind of pawn thrust is profitable and another only provokes weaknesses, and so on.

You can use one of these three theoretical models when trying to solve exercises. During a chess game, it is practically impossible to do this, because there is no time for it. We must internalize these principles and use them when needed. To do this, we must often play in tournaments and solve chess exercises.

We'll use Kotov's approach (the simplest), mainly seeking weaknesses and paying great attention to piece play, as we did before, for example, when we exploited a hole. This will give us an evaluation of the position and the key for finding the right plan. But what can we do in a position where both players play well and there are no clear weaknesses? There is a general principle.

When you have to look for a plan, think first about what kind of pawn thrust you should be aiming for. If no pawn thrust is in prospect, ask yourself what to undertake with your pieces.

Nikolozi Kacharava 1939
Yaroslav Remizov 2088
European Youth Chess Championship
Porec 2015 (U12 Open)

1.e4 d6 2.d4 ♘f6 3.♘c3 e5 4.♘f3 ♘bd7 5.♗c4 ♗e7 6.0-0 0-0 7.♖e1 a6 8.a4 b6 9.♗a2 ♗b7 10.♕e2 c6

What is your evaluation of the position? What is a possible plan for White?

Black played a variation of the Philidor Defence that involves the fianchetto of the queen's bishop and queenside pawn expansion.
Let's remember Kotov's four points:
   1) **Open lines and diagonals;**
   2) **Pawn structure and weak squares;**
   3) **Piece position;**
   4) **Space and the centre.**
White has more space in this position, and the lines for the two bishops are open. Black is more passive, but White must act quickly, as Black is almost ready for counterplay. Regarding weaknesses, Black's weakness on f5 is evident, especially now that the ♗c8 has been fianchettoed. We can say that White must act on the kingside, exploiting if possible the f5-square weakness.

White doesn't have any pawn thrusts at the moment, so he must play with the pieces. But before putting the knight on f5, it is necessary to stabilize the centre.
11.dxe5! dxe5?!
11...♘xe5 was better, not yet closing the centre. For example: 12.♘xe5 dxe5 13.♗e3 b5, with only a small plus for White, as Black can exploit the b4-square with his bishop after 14.f3 ♗b4.
12.♖d1
This move was not strictly necessary, as on 12.♘h4, 12...♘xe4 is risky after 13.♘xe4 ♗xh4 14.♖d1. Anyway, it is a good move. The rook will be useful on the open d-file.
12...♕c7 13.♘h4 ♘c5
13...♗b4 14.♘f5
14.♘f5 b5 15.♗g5
15.♗e3 was better: 15...b4? 16.♕c4! ♘e6 17.♘d5+−
15...b4 16.♘b1 ♔h8
Black could continue with 16...♘xa4 17.♗xf7+ ♖xf7 18.♘xe7+ ♕xe7 19.♖xa4 a5, with a small plus for White.
17.♘xe7 ♕xe7 18.a5 ♘e6 19.♗xe6 ♕xe6 20.♘d2 c5

What is your evaluation of the position? An update of the old plan or a new plan?

Two knights and two bishops have been exchanged. By pushing the pawns, Black has left some weaknesses on his queenside. White's bishop is good, while Black's bishop is rather bad, as it is limited by the white pawn. The ♙a5 can't be successfully attacked, but White can use it for exploiting Black's weakness on b6. Nothing special is happening on the kingside. Hence, the position is clearly better for White. It's time for a new plan, this time on the queenside. White can exploit the c4-weakness with the knight or the queen, and attack the ♙c5 by playing ♗e3. Before playing ♗e3, White must protect his e4-pawn.

21.f3!

21.♗e3 ♘xe4 22.♘xe4 ♗xe4 23.♗xc5 ♕g6 24.f3 ♖fc8 is less clear.

21...♖ad8

A clever try was 21...♗c6 22.♕c4 ♗b5 23.♕xc5 (or 23.♕xe6 fxe6 24.♘b3 ♖ac8 25.♗e3 ♘d7 26.♖d6) 23...♖fc8 24.♕xb4 ♖xc2 25.♘b1, with advantage to White.

22.♗e3 ♘d7 23.♘c4 ♕c6

How can White continue?

Here, White played 24.♕d2?!, and after some mistakes by both sides, probably due to time pressure, the game ended in a draw.

Best was the simple 24.♖d6 ♕c7 (24...♕b5 25.♖ad1 ♗c6 26.♕d3 ♖c8 27.♘b6 ♘xb6 28.♕xb5 ♗xb5 29.axb6 f6 30.♗xc5 ♖xc5 31.b7+−) 25.♖ad1 ♘f6 (25...♗c6 26.♕d2 f6 27.♘b6 ♖f7 28.♗xc5 b3 29.c4) 26.♖xd8 ♖xd8 27.♖xd8+ ♕xd8 28.♗xc5+−.

Teodora Rogozenco   1974
Jasmin-Denise Schloffer   1762
World Youth Chess Championship
Durban 2014 (U14 Girls)

1.d4 ♘f6 2.c4 e6 3.♘c3 ♗b4 4.♘f3 b6 5.♗g5 h6 6.♗h4 ♗b7 7.e3 ♗xc3+ 8.bxc3 d6 9.♗d3 ♘bd7 10.♕c2 ♕e7 11.e4 e5 12.0-0 0-0 13.♖fe1 ♖fd8 14.h3 ♘f8 15.♗g3 ♘g6 16.♘h4 ♘xh4 17.♗xh4 ♔h8 18.f4

White is attacking. How must Black react?

A) Best is 18...exf4 19.e5 dxe5 20.dxe5 (20.♖xe5 ♕d6=) 20...♖xd3! 21.♕xd3 ♕c5+ 22.♗f2 ♕c6, exploiting the light squares and threatening mate. White must enter into a nearly equal endgame after 23.♕f3 ♕xf3 24.gxf3 ♘h7 25.e6 ♘g5 26.exf7 ♘xf3+ 27.♔f1 ♘h2+ 28.♔e2 ♖f8;

B) It is risky to play 18...g5?! 19.fxg5 ♘h7 20.♖f1 ♘xg5 21.♔h1 ♖g8 22.d5.

18...罝e8

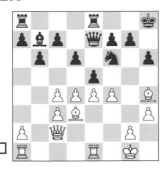

What is your evaluation of the position? What is a plan for White?

1) Open lines and diagonals: White can open the f-file, and in this way increase the pressure on the ♘f6, which is already under observation by the ♗h4;

2) The pawn structure and weak squares: White has doubled pawns, but at the moment they are safe. The four central pawns seem strong enough;

3) Piece placement: White's ♗d3 is rather passive. It's possible, therefore, if White is unable to find a better place for his bishop or to eliminate the ♟e5, that it will be difficult for White to make progress;

4) Space and the centre: White has more space and can easily move his pieces from one side to the other. We can conclude that White has better prospects and that there are two plans: closing the position with 19.f5 or leaving it open with another move. The first possibility is less challenging. White will have a quiet life, without much calculating, but the same goes for Black. To play 19.fxe5, opening the position, or another move requires a greater effort. White must calculate much more, but it's clear that in this way White's pieces will be more active, and it will be more difficult for Black to defend.

> Psychology plays an important role in positional play, as it can change the decision. Sometimes, it makes sense to choose a continuation that is not objectively the strongest, for example, as perhaps in this case, and make things easier. You save time, don't take risks at all and continue to keep up the pressure. This is called 'practical play'. Anyway, I suggest that you, between two more or less equivalent possibilities, choose the more challenging one. Accept complications! Only in this way can you see your limits, improve them and improve your understanding of the game. Moreover, don't accept or offer quick draws!

19.f5

19.fxe5 dxe5 20.罝f1 was better. For example: 20...g5 21.♗g3! (removing the ♟e5) 21...exd4 22.cxd4 ♘xe4 23.罝ae1 f6 24.♗f2 f5 25.d5 c5 26.罝e2 ♚g8 27.♗e1, with a strong initiative.

What is a plan for Black?

19...g6

A strange move, but not a mistake. It was possible to play 19...g5 immediately (20.♗f2 ♖g8), building a barrier on the dark squares (the ♗d3 is blocked). It was also possible to play a waiting move, but probably before or after, Black would have to play ...g7-g5 anyway. For example: 19...♗c6 20.d5 ♗d7 21.g4 a5 22.♖f1 ♖f8 23.♕c1 (23.♕d2 ♖g8 24.♔h1? ♘xe4) 23...♖g8 24.♔h1 ♕f8 25.♕e3 ♘h7, and Black is passive.

20.♖e2 g5 21.♗f2 ♘h5 22.g3 ♖g8 23.♔h2 ♘f6 24.♖ee1 g4 25.h4

25...h5?!

Now, a new weak square emerges: g5. Better was 25...♖ae8. For example: 26.♗e3 ♔h7 27.d5 ♘d7 28.♕c1 ♕f8, and Black is not worse.

26.♖ab1 ♘d7

27.f6!?

Teodora understands that it is not enough to have a space advantage (for example: 27.♕c1 ♔h7 28.♗e3 f6), and decides to sacrifice a pawn to open the f-file. The game continued with

27...♕xf6 28.♖f1 ♕g6 29.♗e3 f6 30.♖f5 ♗c8 31.♖bf1 ♖f8 32.♖5f2 ♗b7 33.♕a4

33...♕h7

33...♗xe4 34.♗xe4 ♕xe4 35.♕xd7 ♕xe3 36.♖f5 ♔g8 37.♖xf6 ♕e2+ 38.♔g1 ♕e3+ 39.♔g2 ♕e2+ 40.♔g1=

34.♖f5 a6 35.♖1f2 ♖ad8 36.♕d1 ♕g6 37.♕f1 ♖f7 38.♗g5 ♖df8 39.♔g1 c5 40.d5 ♔g7 41.♕c1 ♔h7 42.♕f1

42.♗e3

42...♔g7

42...♗c8! 43.a4 ♔g8 44.♗e3 ♘b8 45.♖b2 ♗xf5 46.exf5 ♕g7 47.♖xb6 ♖d8

43.♗e3 ♗c8 44.♖b2

44...♘b8?

It seems that White can do nothing if Black simply waits, for example: 44...♔h8 45.♗c2 ♔g8 46.♗a4?! b5 47.cxb5 ♘b6 48.♗c2 axb5 49.♖xb5 (49.♕xb5?! ♖b7) 49...♗a6

45.♖xb6 ♗xf5 46.exf5 ♕h7 47.♖xd6 ♖c8 48.♕b1 ♖e7?

Now, f6 is weak. Better was 48...♕h8 49.♗e4 ♕f8.

49.♗e4 ♕g8

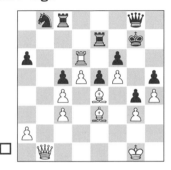

How should White continue?

50.♕b6

This move is enough for winning, but better was 50.♖xf6! ♔xf6 51.♗g5+ ♔f7 52.d6 ♖d7 53.♗d5+.

50...♕f7?

A blunder. Better was 50...♖f7 51.♗g5 ♖cf8 52.♕xc5+−.

51.♗h6+ 1-0

After six rounds of the 2016 World Championship (U12 Girls), Russian Bibisara Assaubayeva was clear first with 5.5 out of 6. Assaubayeva was the great favourite for the tournament, having an Elo of 2287, 161 points more than the second seed. Her opponent in the seventh round was Iranian Motahare Asadi (1980 Elo), one of seven players with 5 points. Clearly, Bibisara played for a win.

Motahare Asadi 1980
Bibisara Assaubayeva 2287
World Cadets Chess Championship
Batumi 2016 (U12 Girls)

1.♘f3 ♘f6 2.g3 g6 3.♗g2 ♗g7 4.0-0 0-0 5.d3 d6 6.c4 ♘c6 7.♘c3 e5 8.e4 h6 9.h3 ♗e6 10.♗e3 ♘d7 11.♘d5 ♘e7 12.♘h4 c6 13.♘c3

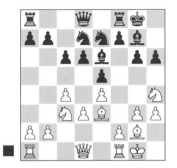

What is your evaluation of the position? What is a feasible plan for Black?

It seems that the position is equal, if not for the fact that Black, taking advantage of the unlucky position of the ♘h4, can improve the placement of her ♘e7. Black has a slight plus.

Both players want to attack on the kingside. It's clear that Black has to push a pawn, but which one?

13...g5!

Playing 13...f5?! would have permitted White to justify the position of the knight. After 14.exf5 ♘xf5 (14...gxf5 15.f4, and White's king is safer than Black's king) 15.♘xf5 (not 15.♘xg6 ♘xe3 16.fxe3 ♖xf1+ 17.♕xf1 ♕g5 18.♘h4 ♕xg3) 15...gxf5 16.f4, the game would be more or less equal.

14.♘f3

Interesting, but doubtful, was 14.f4?! exf4 15.gxf4 gxf4 (15...gxh4 16.f5) 16.♖xf4 ♘g6 17.♘xg6 fxg6 18.♖xf8+ ♘xf8, and Black is better.

14...f5 15.exf5 ♘xf5 16.g4

White didn't want to play passively with 16.♗d2, and invited Black to trade pieces and simplify the position.

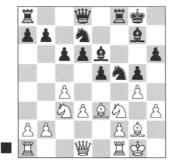

What is your move?

16...♘e7

I suppose the Russian girl played this way to hold the tension. Probably 16...♘xe3 was more precise, but after 17.fxe3 d5 (having the two bishops, it's logical to open the position) 18.cxd5 cxd5 19.♕e2 ♕b6 20.♘d2, Black has a small plus, but with an open position, she must be very careful. This was what Bibisara wanted to avoid. It seems that 16...♘xe3 was the best theoretical move and 16...♘e7 the best practical move. Did Black choose well? It seems so, as her opponent has a lost position in a few moves.

17.♕c2 d5 18.cxd5?!

Not only does this leave Black with control of the important d5-square, but also White must pay attention to an eventual ...♖c8. When we make a pawn exchange, we must avoid improving the pawn structure of our opponent! Better was 18.♘e2 b5 19.b3.

18...cxd5 19.♗xg5?!

White is already worse, but it was worth trying 19.♘b5. For example: 19...d4 20.♘c7 ♖c8 21.♘xe6 ♖xc2 22.♘xd8 dxe3 23.♘e6 e2 24.♖fb1 ♖f6 25.♘xg7 ♔xg7 26.♘e1 ♖d2 27.b4, and Black is better, but White can fight.

19...hxg5 20.♘xg5 ♗f7 21.♘xf7 ♖xf7 22.♘xd5 ♘c6 23.♘e3

23.♖ae1 ♘d4 24.♕c4 b5 25.♘e7+ ♕xe7 26.♕xd4 exd4 27.♖xe7 ♖xe7 28.♗xa8 ♘c5

23...♘d4 24.♕d1 ♘f8 25.a4 ♘fe6 26.♗d5 ♘f4 27.♗xf7+ ♔xf7 28.♘g2 ♘xh3+ 29.♔h2 ♘f4 30.♘xf4 exf4 31.♕c1 ♕h4+ 32.♔g1 ♕xg4+

White resigned.

Assaubayeva won the gold medal with 10 out of 11, Asadi finished fourth with 8.

Javier Habans Aguerrea   1544
Spyros Hartofylakas   1254

European Youth Chess Championship
Prague 2016 (U8 Open)

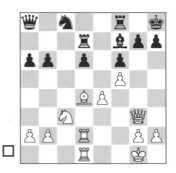

What is your evaluation of the position? What is a good plan for White?

White is superior in the centre, and his pieces are better placed. Black's position is cramped, with many weaknesses. White has a clear plus.

White must act on the kingside. Here, Black has the ♟f6. Such an advanced pawn, if it can be challenged usefully, is called a 'hook'. How can White challenge it in the most effective way? It's simple: put the queen on h4 and push the g-pawn. This was the plan chosen by little Javier.

27.♕h4! ♗g8

After 27...b5, White can attack the weak h7-square with 28.♖d3! (28. a3 ♗c4 29.g4 ♘e7 30.g5 ♘c6 is less promising; 28.♗xf6 gxf6 29.♕xf6+ (29.♖d3? ♕a7+ 30.♔h1 ♗c4−+) 29...♔g8 30.♕g5+ ♔h8 31.♕f6+ ♔g8=). For example: 28...♕c6 29.♖h3 ♗g8 30.♘d5 ♕c2 31.♖e1, with the idea of ♘d5-f4-e6.

28.g4

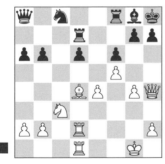

What is the best defensive plan for Black?

28...♕b7?

A) Black had to try to remove the strong ♗d4, and at the same time exchange or improve his worst-placed piece: 28...♘a7! 29.g5 (29.♗xb6 ♘b5, and Black has some

compensation, due to White's exposed king) 29...♘c6 30.g6 (30.♗xb6 ♘e5) 30...♘xd4 31.♖xd4 h6 32.♖xd6 ♖xd6 33.♖xd6 b5 34.a3, and White is better;

B) 28...d5?! 29.g5 fxg5 30.♕xg5 dxe4 31.f6

In a worse position, usually the best plan is to slow down the opponent's attack by simplifying the position. As soon as possible, one needs to prepare a counterattack.

29.♖g2?

A mistake. Much better was 29.g5! fxg5 30.♕xg5 ♖df7 31.♘d5 ♘e7 32.f6 ♘g6 33.fxg7++−.

29...♖ff7?

Again, it was much better to play 29...♘a7! 30.g5 fxg5 31.♕xg5 ♘c6 32.♗e3 ♘e5.

30.g5 fxg5 31.♖xg5 ♘a7

Black found the right plan, but too late. White could now play 32.♘d5! (or 32.♘e2!) ♘c6 33.♘f4, with a decisive advantage. Instead, he played weaker and eventually won in 59 moves.

Shant Sargsyan 2077
Nodirbek Yakubboev 2207
World Youth Chess Championship
Durban 2014 (U12 Open)

1.d4 f5 2.c4 ♘f6 3.♘f3 g6 4.g3 ♗g7 5.♗g2 0-0 6.0-0 d6 7.♘c3 c6 8.d5 e5 9.dxe6 ♗xe6 10.♕d3 ♘a6 11.♗f4 ♘e8 12.b3 ♘c5 13.♕d2 ♕e7 14.♖ad1 ♖d8

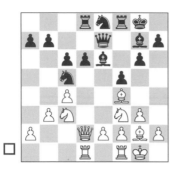

What is your evaluation of the position? What is a good plan for White?

The white pieces are more active than Black's pieces. White has a well-built pawn structure, while Black has a weak d6-pawn. White has at least a small plus.

15.♕e3!

The computer suggests 15.h4, but this doesn't seem to create anything after 15...♗c8 16.♘g5 h6 17.♘h3 ♔h7 18.♗e3 ♘f6. Instead, after 15.♕e3!, White keeps the squares e6, e7 and a7 under control with the queen, and after 15...♘f6 prepares the shot 16.♗xd6! ♖xd6 17.♕xc5. For example: 17...♖fd8 18.♖xd6 ♖xd6 19.♕xa7 ♘e4 20.♘a4, and Black doesn't have enough compensation for the two pawns.

15...♖d7 16.♘d4?!

Better was 16.b4! (a pawn push, against the hook on c6, which is rather common with the pawn structure b7-c6 and the white bishop on g2. After b4-b5-bxc6, Black will have a weak pawn and the white bishop will be more active): 16...♘a6 17.b5 ♘c5 (17...♘ac7 18.bxc6 bxc6 19.♘d4 ♗xc4 20.♗xc6 ♕xe3 21.♗xe3 ♖df7 22.♖d2) 18.bxc6 bxc6 19.♘d4 ♗xc4 20.♕xe7

♖xe7 21.♘xc6 ♖d7 22.♗d5+ ♗xd5 23.♘xd5 ♘e6 24.♗e3, with at least a slight advantage for White.

16...a5?!

Black had to simplify the position with 16...♗f7!. After 17.♖d2 (17.♕xe7 ♖xe7 18.♖fe1 ♖d7) 17...♕xe3 18.♗xe3 ♘f6, the game is nearly equal.

What is your move?

The ♘c5 holds Black's position. So, White has to exchange the best-placed black piece.

17.♘a4! ♘c7?!

Again, it was better to simplify: 17...♗xd4! (17...♘xa4? 18.♘xe6 ♘c3 19.♖d3 ♘xa2 20.♘xf8) 18.♕xd4 (18.♖xd4 ♘xa4 19.bxa4 c5 20.♖d2 ♗xc4 21.♕xe7 ♖xe7) 18...♘xa4 19.bxa4 ♕f6±

18.♘xc5 dxc5

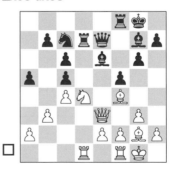

What is your move for White?

19.♘f3

Not bad, but more promising was 19.♘xc6! bxc6 20.♖xd7 ♕xd7 21.♗xc7. For example: 21...♗d4 22.♕f4 a4 23.♗e5 ♖d8 24.e3 ♗xe5 25.♕xe5 ♕d6 26.♕b2

19...♖fd8?!
Black had to try 19...♘a6 20.♖xd7 ♕xd7.

20.♗g5 ♗f6 21.♗xf6 ♕xf6 22.♖xd7 ♖xd7 23.♕xc5 ♕c3 24.e3
24.♕a7! ♘e8 25.♘g5 ♕f6 26.h4 h6 27.♘f3 f4 28.♕xa5

24...♘a6
24...♗f7 25.♘d4 ♘e6 26.♘xe6 ♗xe6 27.♗f3 a4 28.♕a3

25.♕a7 ♕b4?!
25...♖c7 26.♖d1 ♕f6 27.♘d4 ♗c8 28.c5 ♕e7 29.♖c1 a4 30.♗f1+−

26.♘d4
Black resigned: 26...♗f7 27.♗xc6

The following game is rather difficult, but is a very good exercise for tactics, too.

Luis Engel   2166
Mohammed Amin Tabatabaei   2488
World Youth Chess Championship
Halkidiki 2015 (U14 Open)

1.d4 ♘f6 2.♘f3 g6 3.♗f4 ♗g7 4.e3 0-0 5.h3 d6 6.♗e2 b6 7.0-0 ♗b7
This is a rather common variation nowadays. Black usually continues as in the game, leaving the ♖f8 at home, and using the queen to push ...e7-e5 and prepare an expansion in the centre or on the kingside, depending on how White plays.

8.a4 a6 9.♘bd2 ♘bd7 10.c3 ♕e8 11.♕c2 e5 12.dxe5 dxe5 13.♗g3 ♕e7 14.♖fd1 ♖ad8

Both players had spent only a few minutes up to this point.

15.♗c4
White's last move is rather illogical, as now the bishop can easily be attacked with tempo.
15.a5 b5 16.c4 was interesting.

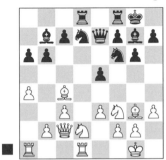

What is your evaluation of the position? What is a good plan for Black?

In practice, a weak move often creates the plan for the opponent or allows him to play a standard plan more effectively. Now, Black will fight to control the d-file and especially the hole on d3. Black now has a slight advantage and the initiative.

15...e4! 16.♘d4 ♘e5 17.♗f1
Or 17.♗e2 ♘d3 18.♗h4 c5.

17...c5?!
This move helps White, as now he can quicky defend the important

d3-hole. Besides, Black's queenside pawns are now weaker. It was better to wait a little bit.

After 17...♘d3 18.♗h4 (18.♘4b3 ♖d7 19.♘c1?! ♖fd8) 18...c5 19.♘4b3 ♕e6 20.♘c1 c4, Black has a slight advantage.

18.♘4b3! ♘h5!? 19.♗h2

19.♘xe4 c4 20.♘d4 ♘d3 21.♘d2! ♘xg3 22.♘xc4 ♘xf2 23.♕xf2 ♘e4!? 24.♕f4 ♗f6, and Black has compensation for the pawn.

19...f5

After 19...♘d3 20.♘c1 ♗e5 21.♘xd3 exd3 22.♕b3 ♗xh2+ 23.♔xh2, the position is nearly equal.

20.♘c4

20...f4?!

Black decides to attack on the kingside, but he should have improved his position earlier and closed the d-file.

Best was 20...♘d3 (if Black doesn't want to take risks, possible is 20...♘xc4 21.♗xc4+ ♔h8, with a small plus for White) 21.♘c1 (21.♘xb6 f4 22.exf4 ♘hxf4 23.♗xf4 ♖xf4 24.♗xd3 exd3 25.♖xd3 ♖xd3 26.♕xd3 ♕e6∓) with an unclear position.

21.♖xd8 ♕xd8

21...♖xd8!? 22.exf4 ♘d3 23.f5 gxf5 24.♘xb6 seems better for White, but it is not completely clear.

22.♘bd2

The idea of attacking the ♙e4 is good, but it was better to play 22.♖d1 first. For example: 22...♕c7 23.♘bd2 b5 (23...♘d3? 24.♘xe4!) 24.axb5 axb5 25.♘xe5 ♗xe5 26.♗xb5 fxe3 27.♗c4+ ♔g7 28.♗xe5+ ♕xe5 29.fxe3 ♘g3 30.♘f1, and White stands better.

22...♘d3 23.♗xd3 exd3

Or 23...♕xd3 24.♕xd3 exd3 25.♗xf4 ♘xf4 26.exf4.

24.♕b3 fxe3 25.♘d6+?

A blunder. After 25.♘xe3+ ♔h8 26.♘dc4, White is slightly better. For example: 26...♖f6 27.♘e5 ♕e8 28.♘xd3

25...♔h8 26.fxe3

How should Black continue?

26...♕e7?

Black was winning after 26...♕g5!. For example: 27.e4 (27.♘xb7 ♕xe3+ 28.♔h1 ♕xd2 29.♕xb6 ♕e2 30.♕d6 d2 31.♖g1 h6–+) 27...♕xd2 28.♘f7+ ♖xf7 29.♕xf7 ♕e3+ 30.♕f2 ♗h6–+

How can White now save half a point?

27.♘f1?

If you found 27.e4!, you are halfway: 27...♗h6

analysis diagram

What should White play now?

White must play actively with 28.♖f1! (28.♘f3 ♗xe4 29.♘xe4 ♕xe4 30.♗e5+ ♗g7 31.♖e1 ♕c6 leaves Black better). The position is equal, and the game would have probably ended with a perpetual check, by White or Black:

A) 28...♗xd2 29.♖xf8+ ♕xf8 30.♗e5+ ♘g7 31.♘f7+ ♔g8 32.♘h6+ ♔h8 33.♘f7+=;

B) 28...♘f6 29.♘xb7 ♗xd2 30.♗d6 ♗e3+ 31.♔h1 ♘h5 32.♖xf8+ ♕xf8

33.♗xf8 ♘g3+ 34.♔h2 ♘f1+ 35.♔h1 ♘g3+=;

C) 28...♘f4 29.♗xf4 ♗xf4 30.♖xf4 ♖xf4 31.♕xb6 ♖f6 32.e5 ♕xe5 33.♕d8+ ♔g7 34.♘e8+ ♔f7 35.♕d7+ ♔f8 36.♘xf6 ♕e3+ 37.♔h1 ♕e1+ 38.♔h2 ♕e5+ 39.♔h1 ♕e1+=

27...♕f6! 28.e4

How can Black continue the attack?

28...h6?

Black loses an important tempo. He was winning with at least three moves:

A) 28...♕f2+ 29.♔h1 ♘f4 (Black played 28...h6, I suppose, because now, after 29...♕xf1+ 30.♖xf1 ♖xf1+ 31.♗g1 d2, White has 32.♘f7+. Black is winning, but must take some risks after 32...♔g8 33.♘g5+ ♔f8) 30.♗xf4 ♕xf4 31.♘xb7 (31.♕e6 ♗e5–+) 31...♕xf1+ 32.♖xf1 ♖xf1+ 33.♔h2 d2 34.♘d8 ♗h6–+;

B) 28...♘f4 29.♗xf4 (29.♘xb7 ♘e2+ 30.♔h1 ♕xf1+ 31.♖xf1 ♖xf1+ 32.♗g1 ♖xg1+ 33.♔h2 ♗e5+ 34.g3 ♗xg3#) 29...♕xf4 30.♘xb7 ♕f2+ 31.♔h1 ♕xf1+ 32.♖xf1 ♖xf1+ 33.♔h2 d2–+;

C) 28...♗c6 29.♘d2 (29.♕d1 ♕f2+ 30.♔h1 ♕xb2 31.♖b1 ♕xc3 32.♖xb6 ♗xa4–+) 29...♕f2+ 30.♔h1 ♕xd2 31.♕xb6 ♘f4 32.♗xf4 ♕xf4–+

29.♕d1!
White defends the first rank. Not
29.♘xb7? ♕f2+ 30.♔h1 ♕xf1+–+.
**29...♕f2+ 30.♔h1 ♗c6 31.♕xd3
♕xb2 32.♖b1 ♕xc3**
Black is better, but won only after a
long battle.

Alejandro Perez Garcia	2165
Timur Fakhrutdinov	2290

European Youth Chess Championship
Batumi 2014 (U14 Open)

**1.♘f3 d5 2.b3 ♘f6 3.g3 c5 4.♗g2
♘c6 5.♗b2 e6 6.e3 ♗e7 7.0-0 0-0
8.c4 b6 9.♘c3 dxc4 10.bxc4 ♗b7
11.♕e2 a6 12.♖fd1 ♕c7 13.♖ab1
♖fd8 14.d3 ♘e8 15.♗a1 ♖ab8 16.h4
h6 17.♘h2 ♘a7 18.♘g4 f5 19.♘h2
♗xg2 20.♔xg2 b5 21.♕h5 ♗f6**

**Try to evaluate the position after
22.♘f3 and after 22.e4.**

White has some problems on the
queenside, and in the meanwhile
has achieved nothing on the
kingside.
22.♘f3?
This loses by force. We already saw
a similar situation when discussing
piece coordination. The queen can
face great dangers when entering
too far into the enemy's camp,
especially if you close her exit.

Much better was 22.e4. For
example: 22...b4 23.♘e2 ♗xa1
24.♖xa1 ♘f6 25.♕f3, with only a
small plus for Black.
22...b4 23.♘e2 ♗xa1 24.♖xa1
24.♘f4 ♖d6 25.♖xa1 ♘f6 26.♘xe6
♖xe6 27.♕xf5 ♕e7 28.d4 ♘e4–+
**24...♘f6 25.♕g6 ♘c6 26.♘f4 ♖d6
27.♘h5**

27...♘e8! 28.♘f4
28.♘xg7 ♕xg7–+
28...♘e7 29.♘xe6 ♕c6 0-1
The white queen was trapped in a
nice way by the Russian boy. Timur
won the gold medal.

Barnabas Persanyi	2237
Dambasuren Batsuren	2214

World School Chess Championship
Iasi 2017 (U13 Open)

**Evaluate the position after 29.♖b1
and after 29.♘c2.**

White decided to fight for the b-file. If you exchange pieces and enter into an endgame, you have to evaluate it correctly. The game went

29.♖b1? ♖ab8 30.♖eb2 ♖xb2 31.♖xb2

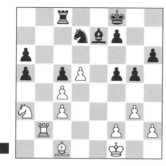

31...♗f6?

Surprisingly, Black doesn't evaluate the endgame correctly, too. After 31...♖b8 32.♖xb8+ ♘xb8, Black would have been clearly better.

32.♖b7 ♚e7 33.♗d2?

33.♖a7 was much better, for example: 33...♗xc3 34.♖xa6 ♖d8 35.♘b5 ♗e5 36.♘a7, with at least a slight advantage for White.

33...♖b8 34.♖xb8 ♘xb8 35.♚e2 ♘d7 36.f4 gxf4 37.gxf4 ♗g7 38.♘c2 ♚f6 39.♚d3 ♚g6 40.♗e3 a4 41.h3 ♗f8

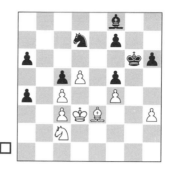

42.♘e1?

After 42.♗c1! ♗d6 43.♘e1 ♘f6 44.♘f3, White retains drawing chances.

42...a3 43.♚c2 a2

This pawn did a good job, and now the white king can't defend the ♙c4. The ♙d5 will fall soon as well.

44.♚b2 ♘b6 45.♚xa2 ♘xc4 46.♗g1 ♘b6 47.♘d3 ♘xd5 48.♚b3 ♗d6 0-1

White had to play 29.♘c2, attacking the black weaknesses and keeping the rooks on the board. After 29...♗f6 30.♘e3 (30.♖xa5?! ♖cb8 gives Black good counterplay. For example: 31.♗a3 ♗xc3 32.♗xc5+ ♚g8 33.♖a3 ♖b1+ 34.♚g2 ♗b2 35.♖a5 ♗c3 36.♖a3 ♗b2=) 30...♗xc3 31.♖aa2, White is a little better.

Batsuren finished 1st-2nd, taking the silver medal on tiebreak.

CHAPTER 4

Test

Here are forty positions for you to solve. You must indicate the correct first move and state the idea behind it. Sometimes, it will be the winning move, other times the drawing move or the move that causes the greatest problems for the opponent.

I suggest that you acquaint yourself with each position, and only after your evaluation of it, decide on the target. It's preferable to use a chessboard and give yourself 10 minutes for each position. A good idea is to solve a few puzzles (five, for example) every day and look at the solutions. By doing this, you can see how well you are going, and you'll learn something that may be possible to apply in the following days.

After a few weeks, try to solve all the puzzles you didn't solve correctly (both the exercises given in the illustrative games and the ones given here), this time giving yourself only five minutes for each one. After a few months, read this book again and try to solve all the puzzles. To learn a skill, it has to be repeated several times.

Exercise 1

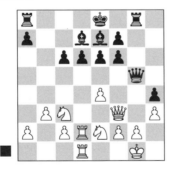

(Solution on page 58)

Exercise 2

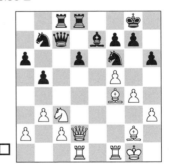

(Solution on page 58)

Exercise 3

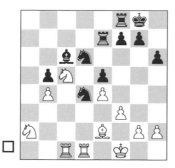

(Solution on *page* 59)

Exercise 4

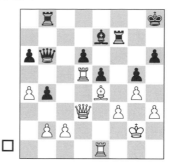

(Solution on *page* 59)

Exercise 5

(Solution on *page* 60)

Exercise 6

(Solution on *page* 60)

Exercise 7

(Solution on *page* 61)

Exercise 8

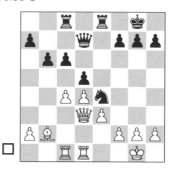

(Solution on *page* 61)

Exercise 9

(Solution on page 62)

Exercise 10

(Solution on page 62)

Exercise 11

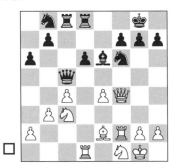

(Solution on page 63)

Exercise 12

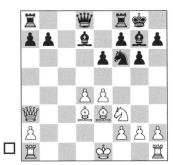

(Solution on page 63)

Exercise 13

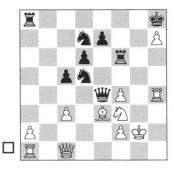

(Solution on page 63)

Exercise 14

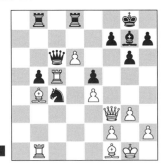

(Solution on page 64)

Exercise 15

(Solution on page 64)

Exercise 16

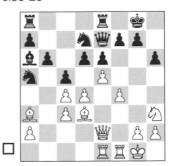

(Solution on page 65)

Exercise 17

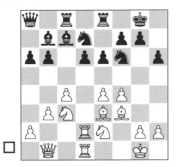

(Solution on page 65)

Exercise 18

(Solution on page 66)

Exercise 19

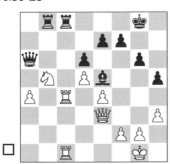

(Solution on page 66)

Exercise 20

(Solution on page 66)

Exercise 21

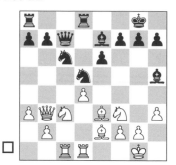

(Solution on page 67)

Exercise 22

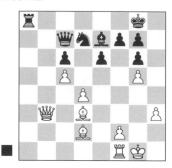

(Solution on page 67)

Exercise 23

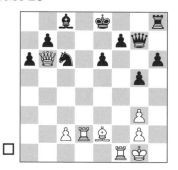

(Solution on page 68)

Exercise 24

(Solution on page 68)

Exercise 25

(Solution on page 69)

Exercise 26

(Solution on page 69)

Exercise 27

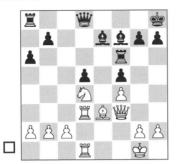

(Solution on page 70)

Exercise 28

(Solution on page 70)

Exercise 29

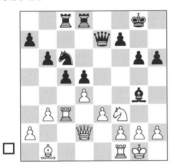

(Solution on page 71)

Exercise 30

(Solution on page 71)

Exercise 31

(Solution on page 72)

Exercise 32

(Solution on page 72)

Exercise 33

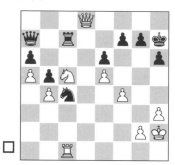

(Solution on page 72)

Exercise 34

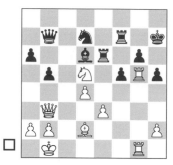

(Solution on page 73)

Exercise 35

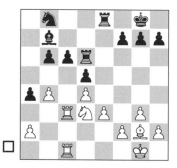

(Solution on page 73)

Exercise 36

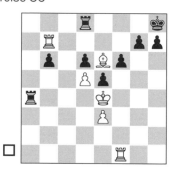

(Solution on page 74)

Exercise 37

(Solution on page 74)

Exercise 38

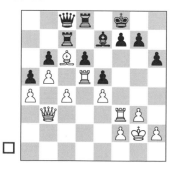

(Solution on page 75)

Exercise 39

(Solution on page 75)

Exercise 40

(Solution on page 76)

CHAPTER 5

Solutions

Solution 1

| **Alireza Firouzja** | 2364 |
| **David Tianjian Peng** | 2231 |

World Youth Chess Championship

Halkidiki 2015 (U12 Open)

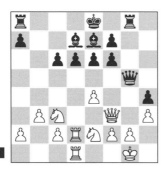

The game continued with

17...e5!

Black wants to eliminate White's ♙e4, and build a very strong pawn centre. At the same time, he opens the diagonal for the ♗d7 and restricts the movements of the ♘e2.

A) It was not possible to play 17...d5?, because of 18.exd5 cxd5 19.♘xd5 exd5 20.♖xd5;

B) 17...c5 is not clear: 18.e5 d5 19.♘xd5 exd5 20.♕xd5 ♖d8 21.♕b7 ♕f5 22.exf6 ♗xf6 23.♔f1;

C) 17...♖d8 is interesting, but only with the idea to improve the position of the ♗c8. For example: 18.♘f4 ♗c8 19.a3 ♗b7

18.♘a4?!

Better was 18.♔h1 f5 19.exf5 ♕xf5.

18...f5 19.c4

White's position is very difficult:

A) 19.exf5 d5!;

B) 19.♘ec3 d5 20.exd5 e4 21.♘xe4 fxe4 22.♕xe4 ♗xh3 23.d6 ♗xg2 24.♕xe7+ ♕xe7 25.dxe7 ♗f3+ 26.♔h2 ♗xd1 27.♖xd1 ♖xe7;

C) 19.♖xd6 fxe4 20.♕xe4 ♗xd6 21.♖xd6 ♗xh3 22.♕xc6+ ♔e7 23.g3 ♖ac8;

D) 19.♘ac3 ♖g6 20.♔h1 0-0-0 21.exf5 ♕xf5, and Black is always much better.

19...fxe4 20.♕xe4 f5 21.f4 fxe4 22.fxg5 ♖xg5 23.♔h1 ♗f5 24.♘ec3 e3 25.♖e2 ♖g3 26.b4 ♗g6 27.♖b2 ♗f7 28.b5 ♗xc4 29.bxc6 ♖c8 30.♖c1 ♖xc6 31.♘e2 ♖g6 32.♘g1 ♗d5 33.♖e1 ♖c4 0-1

Solution 2

| **Anthony Atanasov** | 1766 |
| **Liran Zhou** | 1897 |

World Cadets Chess Championship

Poços de Caldas 2017 (U10 Open)

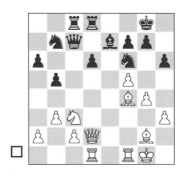

20.♘d5!

White needs the ♗g2 in a much more active position for attacking. The game continued with 20.♘e2?! ♘c5 21.♘d4? (after a prophylactic

move such as 21.♕d4 or 21.♘g3, White is a little better) 21...♘ce4! 22.♕d3 ♘c3 23.♖de1 ♘xa2? (23...♘fd5 24.♗d2 ♗h4 25.♗xd5 ♘xd5∓) 24.♘c6±. The game finished with a draw. The following day, Zhou (USA) won the championship with 9.5/11, a full point ahead of number two, while Atanasov finished seventh.
20...♘xd5 21.♗xd5

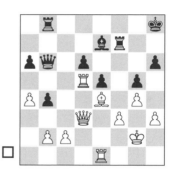

21...♘c5
21...♖e8 22.♗xh6! gxh6? 23.♕xh6
22.g5 hxg5 23.♗xg5 ♖d7 24.f6 ♗f8 25.♖de1
25.♕f4?! ♘e6
25...♕a7 26.♖f2 a5 27.♕f4+−

Solution 3
Monika Marcinczyk   1609
Viktoriia Kirchei   1767
European Youth Chess Championship
Prague 2016 (U12 Girls)

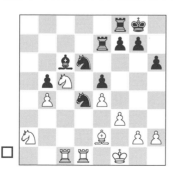

33.♘b3!

The game continued with 33.♖c3?! ♖a8 34.♘c1 ♘xe2 35.♔xe2 ♘c4=.
33...♘xb3 34.♖xc6 ♘c8 35.♗xb5 ♘a7 36.♖b6 ♘xb5 37.♖xb5
With at least a small plus.

Solution 4
Martha Samadashvili   1711
Nusa Hercog   1790
World Youth Chess Championship
Halkidiki 2015 (U12 Girls)

51.a5!
After this move, Black couldn't defend both her weaknesses (a6 and d6). The game continued with 51.♕b3? ♔g7, and the game was still rather unclear, but with better chances for White.
51...♕c7
51...♕a7

analysis diagram

52.♖xd6! ♗xd6 (52...♖f6 53.♖xf6 ♗xf6 54.♕d6 ♔g7 55.♕e6

♖d8 56.♗d3+−) 53.♕xd6 ♕c7
54.♕xh6++−
52.♕xa6 ♖f6 53.♕d3+−

Solution 5

Stefan Pogosyan   2200
Gleb Dudin   1965
European Youth Chess Championship
Prague 2016 (U12 Open)

White had played an interesting
exchange sacrifice, but now made
a mistake by playing c4xd5. Black
could answer this with
14...cxd5!
Only after 14...cxd5! does the c-file
become weak for White. The game
continued with 14...exd5? 15.♗b2
♕a2 16.0-0 (interesting is 16.f3 ♘g3
17.♘c3 ♕xb2 18.♕xb2 ♘xh1, with
unclear play) 16...a5 17.f3 axb4 (17...
a4!? 18.fxe4 a3 19.♘xa3 ♖xa3 20.♗d1
♘xe4) 18.fxe4 ♘xe4 19.♗d3, and
White was not worse.
15.f3
  A) 15.♗d3 0-0 16.♕b2 ♕xb2
17.♗xb2 a5 18.b5 a4 19.b4 ♖fc8−+;
  B) Perhaps Black feared 15.♗b5+?!,
but Black can take the c-file after
15...♔d8!.
**15...0-0 16.fxe4 ♖fc8 17.♕b2 ♕xb2
18.♗xb2 ♖c2 19.♗a3 dxe4!**
Preventing ♗f3.
20.b5 ♖ac8

With great advantage for Black. For
example:
21.♖g1 ♖a2 22.♗c4
22.h3 ♘d5 23.♗f2 ♖cc2−+
**22...♘g4 23.♗c1 ♖a1 24.♔d2 ♖xb1
25.h3 a5 26.bxa6 b5−+**

Solution 6

Can Dolgun   1620
Volodar Murzin   2039
European Youth Chess Championship
Porec 2015 (U10 Open)

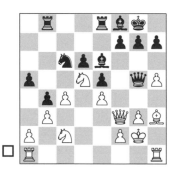

22.h6!
22.♖ad1?! h6
22...♗xh3+
Better was 22...♗xd5 23.cxd5
♘d4 24.♘xd4 exd4 25.hxg7 ♗xg7
26.♖ac1, with advantage for White.
23.♖xh3 ♖e6 24.hxg7 ♗xg7

25.♖ah1
The game continued with 25.♕h5?!
♕g6.

**25...h6 26.♕d3 ♖g6 27.♘ce3 ♔h7
28.♖h5 ♕d8 29.♘f5**
With a great advantage for White.

Solution 7
Dambasuren Batsuren 2072
Aydin Turgut 1884
World Youth Chess Championship
Halkidiki 2015 (U12 Open)

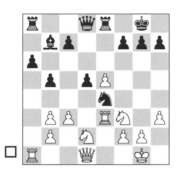

The game continued with
16.b4!
16.♕e2 c5=
16...c5
16...♖e6 17.♘b3 ♖g6 18.♘a5 ♕c8
19.♘d4
17.bxc5 ♘xc5 18.♘b3 ♘a4?!
18...♘e4 19.♘a5 ♕c7 20.♘d4 ♗c8
21.f3±
19.♕e2 ♘b6

20.e6
20.♘a5 ♗c8 21.♘d4 seems a little
better.
20...♘c4?!

20...fxe6 21.♖xe6 ♕d7 22.♘fd4 ♖xe6
23.♘xe6, and White is better.
**21.exf7+ ♔xf7 22.♖xe8 ♕xe8
23.♕d3 ♔g8 24.♖e1**
With a clear advantage to White.

Solution 8
Rutumbara Bidhar 1780
Danitza Vazquez Maccarini 1935
World Youth Chess Championship
Durban 2014 (U14 Girls)

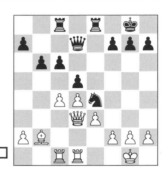

18.♗a3!
Prophylaxis.
 A) The game continued with
18.♖c2? ♘d6! 19.cxd5 cxd5 20.♖xc8
♖xc8 21.♕b3 ♘c4, with a slight
advantage to Black, who got an
interesting initiative on the
kingside after 22.♗c3 ♕g4 23.♖e1
h6 24.a4 ♕e4 25.♗b4 a5 26.♗c3
♖c6;
 B) Another possibility to avoid
18...♘d6 was 18.c5?!, but White
closes the c-file, and Black can
think about some activity on the
kingside, for example with 18...h5
19.f3 ♘g5.
18...♕e6
Or 18...h5 19.f3 ♘g5 20.♖c2 h4
21.h3.
19.♖c2 b5 20.cxb5 cxb5 21.♗c5 a6
With an even game.

Solution 9
Marieta Khachatryan   1449
Eva Stepanyan   1854
World Cadets Chess Championship
Batumi 2016 (U12 Girls)

24...♗a3!
Eliminating the defender. There is no time for another move, for example: 24...♔h8? 25.♖c2 ♗a3 26.♗a1∓
25.♗xa3 ♕xa3 26.c5 bxc5
26...♖c8!?
27.dxc5

And now, instead of 27...♗c6?!, 27...♖c8 was better. For example: 28.♕c3 a5 29.♖f2 ♖d5 30.♖fc2 ♖cxc5 31.♕xc5 ♖xc5 32.♖xc5 e3 33.♖5c2 e2 34.♔f2 ♕d6 35.♔xe2 ♕xf4, with a great advantage to Black.

Solution 10
Martyna Wikar   1803
Busra Ozbek   1660
European Youth Chess Championship
Prague 2016 (U12 Girls)

Maybe something is out of order in Black's position?
24...♕h4!
The game went 24...d5?! 25.cxd5 ♘xd5 26.♘xd5 ♗xa1 27.♖xa1 ♗xd5 28.♗xd5 cxd5=.
25.♖f1 ♖a8
The rook enters into play.
26.e4

26...♕d8!
Now, everything is OK (not 26...g5?! 27.f5 ♗c8 28.♘f3=). After 27.♗b2 (27.b5 g5!) 27...g5! 28.♘d1 ♗xb2 29.♘xb2 gxf4 30.♖xf4 ♖a2, Black is better.

Solution 11
Svitlana Demchenko   1985
Elizaveta Solozhenkina   2248
World Youth Chess Championship
Montevideo 2017 (U14 Girls)

___

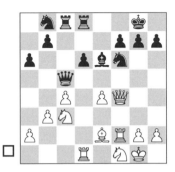

22.♘d5?!
The d6-pawn is isolated, difficult to defend, and it cannot be safely advanced. Being on a half-open file, as in this case, worsens the situation, as the pawn could be easily attacked by White's rooks and queen. White has another option, namely to place a knight on the hole in front of the pawn, without any risk of a pawn driving it away. Hence, there is no reason for White to close the d-file with one of her pawns. Instead of the move played, it was better to bring the other knight into play, which allows White to take on d5 with one or two pieces, according to needs, and leave the d-file open: 22.♘e3 ♔h8 23.♘cd5 ♘bd7 (23...♗xd5 24.♘xd5 ♘bd7 25.♘e7 ♖b8 26.♘f5) 24.b4 ♕a7 25.♘e7 ♖a8 26.♖xd6 (26.♘7f5 ♗xf5 27.♘xf5 g5 28.♕e3 ♕xe3 29.♘xe3±) 26...♖e8 27.♘7f5 ♗xf5 28.♘xf5 ♖xe4 29.♕d2, with a complicated position where White is slightly better.
22...♗xd5 23.exd5 ♖e8 24.♘g3 ♘bd7 25.♗d3 ♘e5 26.h3

And now best is 26...b5!, with chances for both sides.

Solution 12
Jonas Eilenberg   1634
Timothe Razafindratsima   1938
European Youth Chess Championship
Prague 2016 (U10 Open)

___

14.♘e5!
In the game, Black took the initiative after 14.0-0 ♗c6! 15.♘d2 ♘g4.
14...a6! 15.0-0 ♗b5 16.♖ac1 ♘e8 17.♖fd1 ♘d6 18.♗f4
With a small plus to White.

Solution 13
Mamikon Gharibyan   2263
Yuhao Cai   1860
World Cadets Chess Championship
Batumi 2016 (U12 Open)

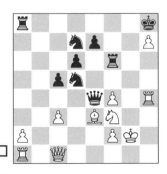

24.♕b1!

The game continued 24.♔g3?! ♖g6+ (24...e5! 25.♕b1! exf4+ 26.♗xf4 ♕xb1 27.♖xb1 ♖af8 28.♗xd6 ♖xd6 is probably better) 25.♘g5 ♖f8?! (25... e5! 26.♕b1!∓), and White could have obtained a small plus with 26.♖g4 ♕d3 27.♕b1. I suppose White played 24.♔g3 because he didn't evaluate the position correctly. With a king so badly placed, he had to try to exchange the most dangerous black piece, even if this would mean losing his material advantage.

24...♘xe3+

Black risks staying worse after other moves. For example:

  A) 24...♕xb1 25.♖xb1 ♘xc3 26.♖b7 ♘f8 27.♖h5±;

  B) 24...♖g6+?! 25.♔h2 ♕xb1 26.♖xb1 ♘xc3 27.♖b7 ♘f6 28.f5 ♖g7 29.♘g5

25.fxe3 ♕xe3 26.♕e1! ♕d3

26...♕xe1 27.♖xe1 ♖xa2+ 28.♔g3, and the game is nearly even.

27.♘g5 ♖af8 28.♕g3

With chances for both sides.

Solution 14

Angel Hernandez-Camen   2046
Florian Mesaros   2201

World Youth Chess Championship

Durban 2014 (U14 Open)

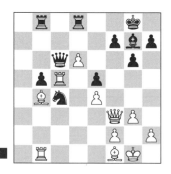

We said that, before exchanging, you should focus more on which

pieces remain on the board than on the ones you exchange. This is true for the queen, too.

35...♕xd6!

  A) After 35...♕e8?! 36.♖d5 ♗f8 37.♖bd1 ♕e6 38.♗xc4 bxc4 39.♕c3 h5 40.h4, White is better;

  B) The game continued with 35...♕a6? 36.♖c7 f6 37.♕c3 ♔h8? (37...♘xd6 38.♖a1 ♕b6 39.♖aa7 ♘e8 40.♗a5 ♕e6 41.♖xg7+ ♘xg7 42.♗xd8 ♖xd8 43.♕c7+–) 38.♖a1 ♕b6 39.♗c5 1-0.

36.♖xc4

36.♗xc4 bxc4 37.♖xc4 ♕e6=

36...bxc4 37.♗xd6 ♖xb1 38.♕a3 c3 39.♕a2 ♖b2

39...♖xf1+ 40.♔xf1 ♖xd6 41.♕a8+ ♗f8 42.♕c8 ♖d1+ seems a draw as well.

40.♕a3 ♖b1 41.♕a2 ♖b2=

Solution 15

Florian Mesaros   2201
Mihnea Costachi   2356

World Youth Chess Championship

Durban 2014 (U14 Open)

This time you had to find the only move that causes some problems for Black, although probably not enough to draw. White has a great hole on g4 and must fight for this square. Black's knight can't go there without being traded.

25.♗f1!
The game continued with 25.♘bd1?
♗xe2 26.♘xe2 ♘g4+ 27.♔g2 ♕c2
28.♘ec3 ♘xf2 29.♘xf2 ♗d2 30.♕e2
♕xc3, and White resigned after a
few moves.
25...♗f3
25...♗d7 26.♗e2 ♘g4+ 27.♗xg4
♗xg4 transposes.
26.♗h3! ♘g4+
It's better to return to the previous
position with 26...♗g4 27.♗f1,
and now Black must find a good
idea. The best idea seems to be to
change flanks and attack on the
queenside (not easy to find when
you are concentrating on attacking
the opponent's king) with 27...b5
28.a3 ♗d7 29.♗e2 a5 30.bxa5 ♖xa5
31.♘d3, and White can fight, too.
27.♗xg4 ♗xg4 28.♘bd1!
Not 28.♖g2 ♘e8!, with an eye to g4.
**28...♗xd1 29.♘xd1 ♕g4 30.♗e3
♗xe3 31.♕xe3 ♖f3 32.♕e1 ♖af8
33.♖g2 ♘e8 34.♘f2 ♕d7**
Black is better, but the game is open.

Aiming for the weak d6-square.
16...d5
16...♗b7 17.♘e4 ♗xe4 18.♗xe4
♖ac8 19.♖f3 ♘f8 20.♖ef1, with a
dangerous attack.
17.cxd5 ♗xd3 18.♘xd3
18.♕xd3 exd5 19.♕f3 ♘c4 20.♗c1
was less good.
18...exd5

19.♕g4
The game continued with 19.f5?!
♘f6.
19...♖ac8
Or 19...♘c4 20.♗c1.
20.f5 ♕g5 21.♕f3
With a strong attack.

Solution 16
Ariel Erenberg 2308
Semen Elistratov 2227
European Youth Chess Championship
Batumi 2014 (U14 Open)

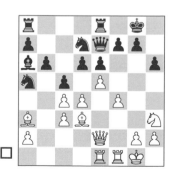

16.♘f2!

Solution 17
Sebastian Lukas Kostolansky 2015
Arsen Davtyan 1752
European Youth Chess Championship
Prague 2016 (U10 Open)

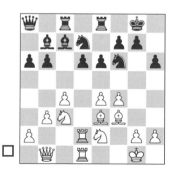

20.g4?

A) It was necessary to prevent 20...b5 with 20.a4. For example: 20...♘c5 21.♘g3 ♗c6 22.b4 ♘cd7 (22...♘xa4? 23.♘xa4 ♗xa4 24.e5) 23.b5 axb5 24.axb5±;

B) Possible, but less clear, was 20.♘g3 b5!? 21.cxb5 ♗a5 22.bxa6 ♗xa6 23.e5 ♗b7 24.♗xb7 ♕xb7 25.exf6 ♗xc3 26.♘e4 ♗xd2 27.♖xd2 ♖c6 28.♘xd6 ♖xd6 29.♖xd6 ♘xf6. White's 20.g4 is very risky, but Black played mechanically:

20...♖ed8?!

Instead of 20...b5! 21.cxb5 axb5 22.a3 ♗c6 23.♖a2 ♕b7, with at least a slight advantage to Black.

Solution 18

Zuzanna Rejniak 1381
Evita Cherepanova 1675

European Youth Chess Championship

Prague 2016 (U10 Girls)

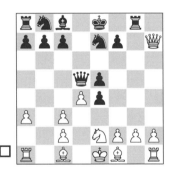

12.♘g3!

Developing the pieces and preventing 12...♗f5. In the game, White was materialistic and played 12.♗b2?!. After 12...♗f5 13.♕h4?! (better was 13.♕h6 ♘d7 14.0-0-0 0-0-0, with a small plus to White) 13...♘bc6 14.♘g3 0-0-0, Black was a little better.

12...exd4 13.c4

13.cxd4 ♕xd4 14.♖b1 was another good possibility for White.

13...♕e6 14.♕xe4 ♘d7 15.♕xe6 fxe6 16.h4 e5 17.♗g5

And White is clearly better.

Solution 19

Bogdan Kalabukhov 2090
Lance Henderson de la Fuente 2306

European Youth Chess Championship

Prague 2016 (U14 Open)

Is the c8-square well-defended or not?

27.♕a7!

The game went 27.g3? ♖xc4 28.♖xc4 ♕a5 29.♔g2 ♗f6 30.♕a7?? ♖xb5, and Black won!

27...♖xc4 28.♕xb8+ ♔g7 29.♖xc4+−

Solution 20

Andreas Garberg Tryggestad 2161
Francesco Sonis 2427

European Youth Chess Championship

Prague 2016 (U14 Open)

The previous move was ♘a4. If Black had a bishop on c2, it could attack two white pieces.

16...f5!

A) There is no time for 16...♖hf8? 17.♘b6+ cxb6 18.♖xd6 f5 19.♖fd1 ♖f7 20.exf5 ♖fe7 21.♘c3, with advantage to White, as in the game;

B) 16...♗e6 17.b3 gives White a small plus.

17.exf5 ♗xf5 18.g4 ♗xc2

Interesting, but very complicated, was 18...♗xg4 19.fxg4 ♘f6 20.h3 ♖hf8. For example: 21.♗d4 c5 22.♘xc5 ♗xc5 23.♗xc5 ♘e4+ 24.♔g2 ♘xc5=

19.♘b6+ ♔b8 20.♖xd6

20.♘d7+ ♔c8 21.♘b6+ ♔b8=

20...cxd6 21.gxh5 ♗d3 22.♖g1 ♗xe2 23.♔xe2 ♖e7 24.♔f2 ♖he8

With a roughly even game. For example:

25.♘c4 d5 26.♗f4+ ♔a7 27.♗e3+ ♔b8=

Solution 21

Justin Wang 2046
Oskar Oglaza 2118
World Youth Chess Championship
Halkidiki 2015 (U10 Open)

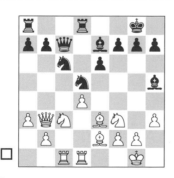

16.♘xd5!
White must exchange the strong black knight and attack the c6- and c7-squares.

A) After 16.♘e4?! ♖ac8 17.♘c5 ♗xc5 18.dxc5 h6 19.♖d2 ♕e7 20.♖cd1 ♖d7, Black is slightly better;

B) Worse is 16.♘b5? ♕b6 17.♕d3 ♗g6 18.♕d2 ♘a5−+.

16...♖xd5?!
Better was 16...exd5 17.g4 ♗g6 18.♘e5, with a small plus for White. For example: 18...♗e4 19.f3 ♗g6 20.♗b5

17.g4! ♗g6 18.♘e5 ♗e4 19.♗f4 ♗d6
19...g5!? 20.♗g3 ♕b6 21.♕xb6 axb6 22.♘xc6 bxc6 23.f3 ♗g6 24.♖xc6

20.♕e3 f6
20...f5 21.gxf5 ♗xf5 22.♗f3 ♖f8 23.♗xd5 exd5 24.♘xc6 bxc6 25.♗xd6 ♕xd6 26.♖c3

21.♕xe4 fxe5 22.dxe5 ♖xe5
22...♗xe5 23.♖xd5 exd5 24.♕xd5+ ♕f7 25.♗c4 ♕xd5 26.♗xd5+ ♔f8 27.♗xe5 ♘xe5 28.♗xb7 ♘d3 29.♗xa8

23.♗xe5 ♗xe5 24.♗d3
With a great advantage to White.

Solution 22

Andrey Esipenko 2490
Jan Pultorak 2296
European Youth Chess Championship
Prague 2016 (U14 Open)

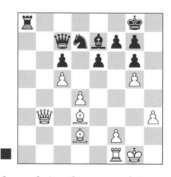

Black exploits the two white weaknesses, d3 and g5, with
32...♕d8! 33.h4 ♗xc5 34.♗xg6
It was slightly better to play 34.♕c4 ♗f8 35.♕xc6 ♘b6 36.♗e3 ♘d5∓.

34...♗xd4 35.♗b1 ♘e5
With advantage to Black.

Solution 23

| **Aleksandra Maltsevskaya** | 2107 |
| **Marika Kostecka** | 1696 |

European Youth Chess Championship
Porec 2015 (U14 Girls)

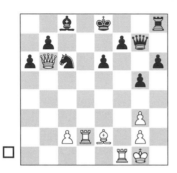

There are different ways to attack Black's weaknesses on the queenside. If you think strategically, you will find the solution.

29.♗f3!
In the game, White played 29.♗xa6?, and after 29...♕c3 30.♗xb7 ♗xb7 31.♕xb7, instead of 31...♕xd2? 32.♕xf7+ ♔d8 33.♕f6+ ♔c7 34.♕xh8+−, Black could simply castle, with a nearly equal game (31...0-0 32.♖df2 ♘e5).

29...0-0 30.♗xc6 bxc6 31.♖d8

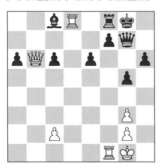

Trapping the bishop.

31...♔h7
31...a5 32.♖xf8+ ♕xf8 33.♖d1+−
32.♖fd1 h5 33.♖xf8 ♕xf8 34.♖d8+−

Solution 24

| **Nikolaz Petriashvili** | 2185 |
| **Aram Hakobyan** | 2348 |

European Youth Chess Championship
Porec 2015 (U14 Open)

The game continued with
16...c5!
Attacking the base of the pawn chain. Too slow is 16...♖fd8 17.♗e4=.

17.♗e4
A) 17.dxc5 ♗xf3 18.♕xf3 ♕xc5 19.♗xb5 ♖xb5 20.♖xd7 ♖xb2 21.♘a4 ♕b5 22.♘xb2 ♕xd7 23.♕e4 ♖c8;
B) 17.♘xb5 ♗xf3 18.♕xf3 cxd4 19.♘xd4 ♘xe5 20.♕e2 ♖fd8, with advantage to Black.

17...cxd4

18.♗xb7

68

18.♘xd4 ♘xe5 19.♘dxb5 ♗a6 20.a4
♖fd8

**18...dxc3 19.♗c6 ♘b6 20.bxc3 ♘a4
21.♕e3 ♕c7 22.♖d6 ♘xc3 23.♘d4
b4**

And Black was clearly better.

Solution 25
Marija Sibajeva 1930
Anna Kochukova 2049
European Youth Chess Championship
Porec 2015 (U14 Girls)

Black has two strong bishops and
threatens to win a piece with
23...♗e5. White must coordinate her
pieces, avoiding a tactical blow and
thereby entering a very difficult
position.

23.♗h3!

The game continued 23.♕d2?? e3!
24.fxe3 ♗xg2 25.♔xg2 ♗e5 26.♘e4
♕b7 27.♕d8+ ♔h7 28.♕d3 f5−+.

23...♕d8

23...♕xh3 24.♘xb7 e3 25.f3 gives
White good drawing chances. For
example: 25...♕c8 26.♘d6 ♕d7
27.♕d3 ♗xb2 28.♘f5 ♕xd3 29.exd3
♔f8 30.♔f1 b5 31.♔e2 g6 32.♘xe3
♔e7 33.♘c2 ♔e6 34.d4 ♗c3 35.♔d3
♗a5 36.♘e3

24.♕d2 ♗xb2 25.♗f5!

White recovers the pawn.

25...♗a3

25...e3 26.♕xe3 ♕xd6?? 27.♕e8+
♕f8 28.♗h7+

26.♗xe4

A similar possibility was 26.♘xe4
♕xd2 27.♘xd2.

**26...♗c8 27.♘c4 ♕xd2 28.♘xd2
♗e6 29.♗d3 ♗b4 30.♘b3 a5
31.♗b5**

With good chances to draw,
although Black is slightly better.

Solution 26
Pedro Antoni Gines Esteo 2194
Faddey Mochalin 2020
European Youth Chess Championship
Prague 2016 (U12 Open)

24...♘f8!

Black improves the knight and
attacks a weakness.

A) The game continued with
24...♖a3?! 25.♖a1! (exchanging
Black's active pieces) 25...♖ha8
26.♖xa3 ♖xa3 27.♖b1 ♖a7 28.♖b2
f4, and now White played 29.♘a2,
which is interesting and gives a
small plus, but it seems better to
play 29.♖a2 ♖xa2+ 30.♘xa2;

B) It was possible, but less
efficient, to improve the other
knight with 24...♘g8 25.♖a1 ♘gf6
26.♗e3 ♖xa1?! 27.♖xa1 ♖xh2 28.♖a7.
This is because a minor piece is
strong if it attacks a weakness

(a rook can be strong in other situations, especially when pushing a pawn).

25.♗d3

25.♖b1 ♘e6 26.bxc6 bxc6 27.♖b6 ♗f6 28.♖xc6 ♗xd4 29.♖xe6 ♗xf2 30.♖a6 ♖xa6 31.♗xa6 ♗xc5 32.♘xd5 g5

25...♘e6 26.bxc6 bxc6 27.♖b1 ♗f6 28.♖b7+ ♔g8 29.♖b6 ♗xd4 30.♖e1 ♗xc5 31.♗xc5 ♘xc5 32.♖xc6 ♘xd3 33.♔xd3 ♔h7

With a roughly even game. For example: 34.♖ee6 ♖hd8 35.♖xg6 d4 36.♘e2 ♘f7 37.♖ge6 ♖a3+ 38.♔d2 ♖a2+ 39.♔d3 ♖a3+

Solution 27

Leya Garifullina   1906
Kseniya Zeliantsova   1723

European Youth Chess Championship
Prague 2016 (U12 Girls)

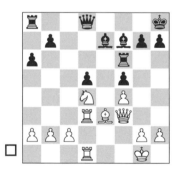

19.♗f2!

In the game, White preferred 19.c3, with only a small advantage.

19...♗g8

19...♕d7 20.♗h4 ♖b6 21.♗xe7 ♕xe7 22.♖e3 ♕c5 23.b3

20.♗h4 ♖f7 21.♗xe7 ♖xe7

21...♕xe7 22.♖e3

22.♘xf5 ♕b6+ 23.♕f2 ♕xf2+ 24.♔xf2 ♖f7 25.♘e3 ♖xf4+ 26.♔g1 h6 27.♘xd5

With a clear advantage to White.

Solution 28

Viktoria Radeva   2150
Ena Cvitan   2007

European Youth Chess Championship
Porec 2015 (U14 Girls)

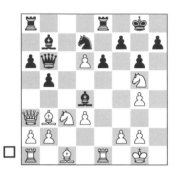

Black threatens 18...b4. White takes the chance to bring her passive queen to the kingside.

18.♕b4!

After 18.♖xe6 fxe6 19.♗xe6+ ♔g7 20.♘ce4 ♘f6 and 18.♘ce4 b4 19.♕a4 ♗c6 20.♘f3 ♗xa4 21.♗xa4 ♖ed8, Black is at least equal.

18...♗xf2+ 19.♔f1 ♗xe1 20.♕f4

20...♖f8

White has a large advantage, both after

A) 20...♘e5 21.♗e3 ♕xd6 22.♖xe1 h6 23.♘ge4 g5 24.♘f6+ ♔h8 25.♕h2 ♔g7 26.♘xe8+ ♖xe8 27.d4 ♘c4 28.♕xd6 ♘xd6 29.d5; and

B) 20...♕f2+!? 21.♕xf2 ♗xf2
22.♔xf2 ♖ad8 23.♗f4.
21.♗e3 ♕c6 22.♘ce4 ♗c3?!
22...♗h4 23.♖c1+−; 22...h6
23.♔xe1+−
23.bxc3 ♔g7 24.♗d4+ e5 25.♗xe5+
And Black resigned.

Solution 29

Yijing Yang	1868
Arnash Bauyrzhan	1930

World Youth Chess Championship
Durban 2014 (U14 Girls)

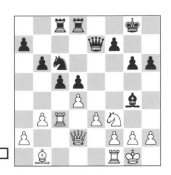

White had to avoid doubled pawns
by playing
18.♘e1!
Other moves leave Black better:
  A) 18.♖fc1? ♗xf3 19.gxf3 ♕g5+
20.♔h1 ♘xd4 21.f4 ♘f3 22.fxg5
♘xd2 23.gxh6 ♘xb1 24.♖xb1 ♔h7
(the game went this way, and Black
won the endgame);
  B) 18.dxc5? ♗xf3 19.gxf3 ♘e5
20.♕e2 ♕f6 21.f4 (21.♖fc1?! ♘xf3+
22.♔h1 ♖e8 23.b4 d4) 21...♘f3+
22.♕xf3 ♕xc3
18...cxd4
  A) Or 18...♕f6 19.h3!, with
complications that seem to give
White at least an equal game:
19...♗d7 (19...♗e6 20.dxc5 d4 21.♖c1
dxe3 22.♕xe3) 20.dxc5 d4 21.♖c1
dxe3 22.fxe3;

B) 18...♕g5 19.h3 cxd4 20.♖xc6
♖xc6 21.hxg4 dxe3 22.♕xe3 ♕xe3
23.fxe3 ♖c3 24.♔f2
**19.exd4 ♕f6 20.♖g3 h5 21.h3 ♗d7
22.♘f3**
With a nearly equal game.

Solution 30

Shant Sargsyan	2441
Ioan Marius Isfan	2011

European Youth Chess Championship
Prague 2016 (U14 Open)

White threatens 34.♖hxh3,
winning. A passive defence, such
as 33...♘e8 34.♖hxh3 ♕f6 35.♖xh6
♖xh6 36.♕g1, leaves White with a
pawn up and a better position. But
perhaps White has important weak
squares?
33...♖e8!
Yes! White has problems on the
e-file. The game went 33...♘h5??
34.♖g8+ ♖xg8 35.♕xh4 1-0.
34.♘g2
34.♕g1 ♖xe3 35.♖gxh3 ♖e1+
36.♔a2 ♖xg1 37.♖xh4 ♖xh4
38.♖xh4 ♖f1=
**34...♕h5 35.♕e2 ♖e7! 36.♘f4
♕e8 37.♖gxh3 ♖xh3 38.♖xh3 ♖xe3
39.♕f2 ♖e1+ 40.♔a2 ♕e3 41.♕xe3
♖xe3 42.♗d1 ♔b7**
With only a small plus for White.

Solution 31
Mariya Yakimova 1736
Ayan Allahverdiyeva 2042
European Youth Chess Championship
Mamaia 2017 (U12 Girls)

19...♗g5!
19...♗h4? 20.0-0!±
20.♗xg5?!
20.♘d1 ♗f4 21.0-0 ♕g5∓
20...♕xg5 21.h4 ♕g6 22.♕c5 ♕g4!
22...♖xg2? 23.0-0-0±
23.♕xe5 ♖d8∓ 24.♖h3? ♖xg2
25.♖h1 ♖dd2 0-1
A very nice game by the Azeri girl,
who took third place.

Solution 32
Beloslava Krasteva 2048
Estee Aubert 1800
European Youth Chess Championship
Mamaia 2017 (U14 Girls)

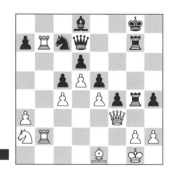

39...♖4g6?

White needs only one move to close
the kingside, and Black permits
her to play that move. Better was
39...h3! 40.♕xh3 (40.g3!? ♗h4 is
complicated, but probably better
for Black) 40...♖xg2+ 41.♕xg2
f3 42.♕xg7+ ♔xg7! (42...♕xg7+?
43.♗g3) 43.♗g3 (43.♘c3 ♗g5;
43.♗a5? ♕a4) 43...♕a4∓.
40.h3 a6
40...a5 41.♘c3± ♖g3 42.♗xg3
♖xg3 43.♕h5 ♖xc3 44.♕g6+
♕g7 (44...♔h8 45.♕h6+ ♔g8
46.♖2b6+−) 45.♕xg7+ ♔xg7 46.♖b8
♗g5 47.♖2b7+−
41.♘c1 ♖f7?!
41...♔h7 42.♘b3±
42.♘b3±

Solution 33
Govhar Beydullayeva 1831
Naomi Bashkansky 1609
World Youth Chess Championship
Halkidiki 2015 (U12 Girls)

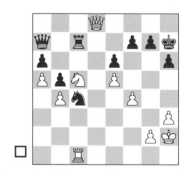

If you find the weakness, you find
the plan.
34.♕f8!!
A beautiful way to exploit a
weakness. White preferred a tactical
shot: 34.♘xa6? ♖d7 35.♕c8 ♕f2?!
(better was 35...♕d4! 36.♔h1 ♖d5.
For example: 37.♕c6 ♘e3 38.♖g1
♕xf4 39.♕c1 ♖xe5 40.♘c5 ♖h5

41.♕d2 ♖d5 42.♕e1 g6–+) 36.♕xd7
♕xf4+ 37.g3 ♕xc1 38.♕d3+ g6
39.♕e2 ♕c3, with more or less even
chances. Black eventually won.

34...♘e3

Or 34...♘d2 35.♖c3!, with the idea of
36.♖g3, aiming for g7! For example:
35...♘e4 36.♘xe4 ♖xc3 37.♘xc3 ♕e3
38.♕c5 ♕xf4+ 39.♔g1 ♕c1+ 40.♔f2
♕f4+ 41.♔e2+–

35.♖c3! ♘f5

35...♘d5 36.♖g3 f6 37.♕d6 fxe5
38.♕xe5 ♖f7 39.♘xe6 ♘f6 40.♕f5+
♔g8 41.♘xg7 ♖xg7 42.♕xf6+–

36.♖d3 ♘h4

36...♖xc5 37.♕xc5+–

37.♖d8

Threatening 38.♖a8.

**37...♖e7 38.g4 ♕c7 39.♕g8+ ♔g6
40.♔g3 ♕c6 41.♔xh4+–**

Solution 34

Alexander Suvorov 2157
Matheo Zachary 2325

European Youth Chess Championship
Mamaia 2017 (U14 Open)

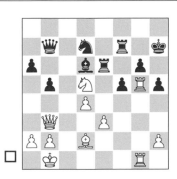

30.e4!

White has two rather inactive
pieces, namely the queen and the
bishop. They must fight on the
kingside. The game continued
with 30.♔a1? ♘f8, and a draw by
threefold repetition after 31.h3 ♕d7

32.a3 ♕e8 33.♗b4 ♗xb4 34.axb4
♖a7 35.♖xh5+ gxh5 36.♘f6+ ♖xf6
37.♕g8+ ♔h6 38.♕g5+ ♔h7 39.♕g8+
♔h6 40.♕g5+ ♔h7 41.♕g8+.

30...f4

A) 30...fxe4? 31.♕h3 ♘f8 32.♖xh5+
♔g7 33.♖h8 ♕xd5 34.♕h6+ ♔f6
35.♗g5++–;

B) 30...♗xh2 31.♖1g2 fxe4 32.♕h3
♖f1+ 33.♗c1+–

31.♕f3 ♘f8 32.e5

White has full control of the board;
for example:

32...♗b8

32...♗e7? 33.♖xh5+

**33.♗xf4 ♔h8 34.♕g2 ♖g7 35.♘f6
♕xg2 36.♖5xg2+–**

Solution 35

Or Globus 2271
Vugar Manafov 2204

European Youth Chess Championship
Mamaia 2017 (U14 Open)

22.b5!

A strong pseudo-sacrifice. In the
game, White obtained only a small
advantage after 22.♖a3?! ♗a6 23.♘b2
b5.

22...♔f8

22...cxb5 23.♖c7 ♗c6 (23...♗a8
24.♘b4 ♖ed8 25.♗f1 ♘d7
26.♗xb5+–) 24.♘b4 ♗d7
25.♗xd5+–

23.♗h3

This move gains an important tempo. Slightly worse was 23.♗f1 cxb5 (23...g6 24.♘b4) 24.♖c7 ♖e7 25.♘e5 ♗a6 26.♖xe7 ♔xe7 27.♖c7+ ♔e8 28.♖a7 f6 29.♘d3±.

23...♖h6

A) 23...g6 24.♘b4 c5 25.dxc5 bxc5 26.♖xc5 d4 27.exd4 ♖xd4 28.♖c7+–;

B) 23...cxb5 24.♖c7 ♗a8 (24...♖e7? 25.♖xe7 ♔xe7 26.♖c7+) 25.♘b4+–

24.♗f1 ♖d6 25.♘b2 a3 26.♘a4 g6 27.bxc6 ♖xc6 28.♗b5 ♖xc3 29.♖xc3 ♖e6 30.♖xa3+–

Solution 36
Daria Vanduyfhuys 1775
Michelle Katkov 1845
European Youth Chess Championship
Mamaia 2017 (U14 Girls)

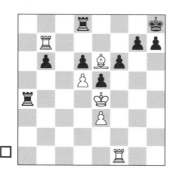

42.♔f5!

Aiming for the ♙d6. In the game, White played less precisely: 42.♔f3?! ♖h4 43.♖b1 g6 44.♖1xb6 f5 45.♖b8?! ♖xb8 46.♖xb8+ ♔g7 47.♖b6 e4+ 48.♔g3 ♖g4+ 49.♔f2, and Black could have fought for a while by playing 49...♔f6.

42...♖a2

A) 42...♖a3 43.♖g1 ♖xe3 44.♖bxg7+–;

B) 42...♖h4 43.♗d7 g6+ 44.♔e6+–
43.♗d7 g6+
43...♖a3 44.♔e6 ♖xe3 45.♔e7 ♖a8 46.♖a1 ♖g8 47.♗e6+–
44.♔e6 f5 45.♗xd6+–

Solution 37
Deshmukh Divya 1993
Amina Kairbekova 1848
World Cadets Chess Championship
Poços de Caldas 2017 (U12 Girls)

19...♘xf3+!

It's not easy to exchange a well-posted knight for a badly-posted bishop, but this is the only way to exploit White's weakness, the d5-pawn (a rather typical situation with these pawn chains that one should remember).

A) 19...f5? was not effective: 20.♗xe5! ♗xe5 (20...fxe4 21.♗xd6 exf3 22.♕xe7 ♗xd5=) 21.exf5 ♖xf5 22.♘e3;

B) The game continued with 19...♘b5?, and White missed 20.♗xe5!, with unclear play. The Indian girl won the game and later the championship with 9.5/11, while the Kazak girl took the bronze.

20.♕xf3 f5 21.♘e3

21.♕h3 fxe4 22.♗h6 ♗xh6 23.♕xh6 ♗xd5

21...e5 22.dxe6 ♘xe6 23.♖xa8!?
23.♕g3 ♘xf4 24.♕xf4 fxe4
23...♖xa8 24.♖xa8 ♕xa8 25.♗xd6
♖d8 26.exf5 ♕xf3 27.gxf3 ♖xd6
28.♘dc4 ♖c6 29.fxe6 ♖xe6∓

Solution 38
Aren Emrikian   1408
Xiaoxi Wei   1453

World Cadets Chess Championship
Poços de Caldas 2017 (U8 Open)

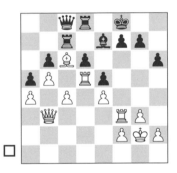

White uses a simple tactic for a
positional purpose, namely to force
a breakthrough for his b-pawn.
41.c5!
Simple and effective.
41...bxc5 42.♖xc5 ♗f6 43.♖cc3 ♕b8
43...♔g8 44.♗d5 ♖f8 45.♖xc7 ♕xc7
46.b6+−
44.b6+−
Aren won the game and afterwards
the tournament, becoming U8
World Champion.

Solution 39
Mani Jahedi   2004
Jonas Bjerre   2375

World Cadets Chess Championship
Batumi 2016 (U12 Open)

16.h4!
The last moment to play actively on
the kingside and avoid remaining
with a backward pawn, that is, a
pawn that is behind all pawns of
the same colour on the adjacent
files and cannot be safely advanced.
The game continued with 16.♕g3?!
♘d7! 17.♖he1 ♘e5 18.h3 ♖c8 19.♖e2
(or 19.♗f1 ♕c5, and Black has
interesting ideas such as ...♖h6-f6-f4)
19...♘c4 20.♖d3 ♗f6 21.♕f2 ♗e5
22.♔b1 ♕c5 23.♘f3 ♕xf2 24.♖xf2
♗f4, with a clear advantage to Black.
16...♘d7!
White has a dangerous initiative
after:
A) 16...gxh4 17.g5 ♘h5 18.g6 ♗f6
19.♗h3 ♗xd4 20.♖xd4; and
B) 16...♖xh4 17.♖xh4 gxh4 18.g5
♘d7 19.g6 ♗f6 (19...♘e5 20.♔b1
♘e5 21.♕h5 ♗f6 22.g7) 20.gxf7+
♔e7 21.♘xe6 ♗xe6 22.♕f5+ ♗xf7
23.♘d5 ♗xd5 24.♕xd5+ ♔g7
25.♕xa8.
17.h5 ♖c8 18.♗f1 ♕b6 19.♗e2 ♗f6
20.♕e3 ♗e5 21.♔b1
With a small advantage to Black.

Solution 40
D Jishitha   2086
Anapaola Borda Rodas   1701

World Youth Chess Championship
Montevideo 2017 (U14 Girls)

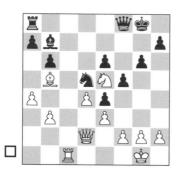

22.♗c6?!

Black's bishop is rather weak, so
there is no need to exchange it.
Better was to gain space with 22.a5!
♖d8 (22...a6!? 23.♗c4 bxa5 24.♕xa5
♕d8 25.♕a3) 23.a6 ♗a8 24.♖c4 ♕d6
25.♕c1 ♔g7 26.h4 h6 27.♖c8±.

22...♕e7?!

22...♗xc6! 23.♖xc6 ♖e8±

23.♗xb7?!

After 23.♗xd5! exd5 (23...♗xd5
24.♖c3 ♕a3 25.♕e1 a5 26.♕b1)
24.a5 ♔g7 25.h3 ♖c8 26.♖xc8 ♗xc8
27.axb6 axb6 28.♕e2 ♕d6 29.♕b5,
White's knight is stronger than
Black's bishop, but Black should
hold.

23...♕xb7

With only a slight advantage for
the Indian girl, playing White, who
anyway won the game and later the
championship.

PART II

Tactics

CHAPTER 6

Calculation

There is a moment in a game when the two armies clash against each other and every move can decide the result. It's time for deep calculation. Up to this moment, general rules and planning have had greater importance. Now, the way of thinking changes, and everything becomes much more concrete. The game is won by the player who calculates better and longer variations. But how can you calculate correctly? The following theoretical model (a revised version of Kotov's model) can help:

1) Look at the position, and in particular analyse the consequences of your opponent's last move;

2) If the position is complicated and there are several possibilities, select the candidate moves, that is, the moves that seem worthy of being played, and make a list of them in your mind.
Don't begin to calculate the first move that seems good. However, this is acceptable if you are playing a blitz game or if you are in time trouble. But if you have enough time, you could miss a stronger move or lose time going back and forth between possible moves if you do this.

How can you find the candidate moves? We saw how in the first part: searching for weaknesses, improving the position of your pieces and your pawn structure, making favourable exchanges and not forgetting your opponent's options (prophylactic thinking).

Regarding tactics, we must consider another factor, namely combinative vision (the ability to quickly discover latent tactical ideas). This is the second component of tactical skill, together with calculation technique. You can make use of puzzle books or internet chess tactics training sites for improving your combinative vision;

3) Calculate the forcing moves first: checking moves, captures and threats. If one of these moves works, you often don't have to calculate other moves. Sometimes, forcing moves appear bad at first sight, but hide a combination. Hence, you should consider all forcing moves.

Only in exceptional situations, return to analyse a line that you have already exhaustively analysed, otherwise you'll lose a lot of time going back and forth with your thoughts;

4) Evaluate the final position obtained by playing each candidate move and remember it. Make a comparison and choose the most efficient move;

5) Try to find the opponent's most troublesome response (this process is called falsification);

6) If everything works, make a blunder check before playing a move.
This model can be applied to strategic games, too. In this case, calculation will be less important than reasoning about positional elements.

Let's pass to the practical examples. After four rounds in the 2015 World Youth Chess Championship (U10 Open), three players had a perfect score: highest-rated, Javokhir Sindarov (Uzbekistan, 2299), Justin Wang (USA, 2046) and Praggnanandhaa Rameshbabu (India, 2077).
Praggnanandhaa had won the World Youth Chess Championship (U8) two years previously, and was paired with white against Sindarov.

Rameshbabu Praggnanandhaa 2077
Javokhir Sindarov 2299

World Youth Chess Championship
Halkidiki 2015 (U10 Open)

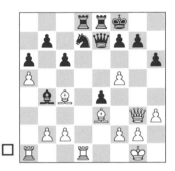

1) **Find sensible candidate moves;**
2) **Choose the strongest one.**

Three reasonable moves have a threat: 22.♗d4 (threatening mate), 22.♕c7 (attacking the ♙b7) and 22.c3 (attacking the bishop). A move like 22.♖d4 seems unable to promise an advantage: 22...♘f6 23.♖xd8 ♖xd8 24.♗b6 ♖d7 25.♕b8+ ♕e8

A) The first possibility, 22.♗d4, gives an equal game after 22...♘f6. For example: 23.♕b3 ♖xd4!? (23...♗d6 24.g3 ♖d7 is possible) 24.♖xd4 ♗c5 25.♖dd1 e3 26.fxe3

♗xe3+ 27.♔h1 ♘g4 28.♖e1 ♘f2+ 29.♔h2 ♘g4+ 30.♔h1;

B) After 22.♕c7, play could continue with 22...♘e5 23.♕xe7+ ♗xe7 24.♗b3 ♖xd1+ 25.♖xd1 ♖d8=;

C) The last chance, 22.c3, allows Black to exchange the bishop. Isn't this bad for White?
The game continued with
22.c3 ♗c5
It seems that the black bishop is well-defended by two pieces, namely the knight and queen, but the Indian boy removes both the defenders with his next two moves.
23.♖xd7! ♖xd7

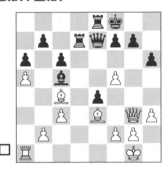

24.f6! ♕xf6
24...gxf6?? 25.♗xh6#
25.♗xc5+ ♔g8 26.♗d4 ♕g5
27.♕xg5 hxg5 28.b4 ♖ed8 29.♗e3
And White won. Praggnanandhaa won the gold medal.

What can you do to learn this skill? Try to play with a computer or a training partner for a certain period, and look for candidates before every move. It will take some time, but gradually this will be internalized and done when needed (of course, in a normal game you need to look for candidates only in particular positions!).

Vincent Keymer   2347
Nodirbek Abdusattorov   2432
World Youth Chess Championship
Halkidiki 2015 (U12 Open)

1) **Find sensible candidate moves;**
2) **Choose the strongest one.**

Black has a clearly better position.
The only chance for White seems to
be a perpetual check.
Regarding candidates, there are
no checking moves and captures
in this position. There is a threat
that was played in the game, which
continued with
38...e3?
Threatening 39...e2.
39.fxe3 f3
It was interesting to play 39...♕e6
(not 39...fxe3 40.♘xe3=), but
if White plays correctly after
40.♕xe6+ ♗xe6 41.exf4 ♗b3 42.g4,
the endgame seems equal. For
example: 42...♗xa4 43.♔g2 ♗xb5
44.♘e3 a5 45.♔f2 a4 46.gxh5+
♔xh5 47.♔e1 a3 48.♘d2 a2 49.♘c2
♗a4 50.♘a1 ♗d7 51.♔c3 ♗xh3
52.♔b2 ♗e6 53.♘c2 ♔g4 54.♘b4
♔xf4 55.♘xa2 ♗xa2 56.♔xa2 ♔e4
57.♔b3
40.g3 f2+ 41.♔h2 ♔h6 42.♕d8 ♔g7
43.♕d7+ ♔g6 44.h4 ♕e4 45.♕d6+
♔g7 46.♕c7+ ♔g8 47.♕d8+ ♔f7

48.♕d7+ ♔g6 49.♕d6+ ♔h7
50.♕c7+ ♔g8 51.♕d8+ ♔f7
52.♕d7+ ½-½

Probably Black, by playing 38...
e3?, didn't see that White could
easily build a fortress for his king.
This was the 38th move. According
to the game score, Nodirbek
had almost 10 minutes for three
moves and used only one minute
for this move. It happens rather
often that a player is short of
time in a tactical position. It is
very important then to be calm
and patient, and to always have a
correct evaluation of the position
(in this case, of the endgame
without queens).
Black, after seeing that 38...e3?
didn't give an easy win, should have
looked for other candidates. One
of these was 38...h4, with the idea
of continuing with 39...e3 40.fxe3
f3, and White doesn't have 41.g3
anymore.
Another possibility was a waiting
move, such as 38...♗e6, to reach the
time control.
The last candidate move was
38...♕e6, to allow, when the White
queen moves, 39...e3 40.fxe3 ♕xh3,
followed by mate.
Having found these moves, which
one had to be examined first?
Clearly 38...♕e6, the most forcing
move. In this case, it is the only
winning move. Let's see:
 A) 38...♕e6! 39.♕c7 (39.♕xe6
♗xe6 40.♔g1 (40.♘d2 e3 41.fxe3
fxe3 42.♘f3 ♔f5 43.♔g1 ♗d5
44.♘e1 ♗b3 45.♔f1 ♗xa4 46.♔e2
♔e4-+) 40...♗b3 41.♘d2 ♗xa4
42.♘xe4 ♗xb5 43.♘d6 ♗d7-+) 39...

e3 40.♘xe3 fxe3 41.♕g3 ♔f5 42.fxe3 ♕g6 43.♕f4 ♔e6 44.♕f2 ♕f5–+;

  B) 38...h4? 39.♕c8 e3 40.fxe3 f3 41.♕g4 ♕g5 42.♕xg5 ♔xg5 43.gxf3 ♗xf3 44.♔g1 ♗d1 45.♘d2 ♗xa4 (45...♔g6 46.♔f2 ♗xa4 47.♘f3 ♗xb5 48.♘xh4 ♔h5 49.♘f3 a5 50.♔e1 ♗d7 51.♔d2 ♗xh3 52.♘d4 ♔g5 53.♔c3 ♔f6 54.♘c6 a4 55.♔b4 ♗d7 56.♘d4 ♔e5 57.♘e2=) 46.♘f3 ♔f5 47.♔f2 ♔e4 48.♘d4 ♗d1 49.♘c6 ♗b3 50.♘xa7 ♗e6 51.♘c6 ♗xh3 52.♘e7 ♗d7 53.♘g6 h3 54.♘e7 ♗e6 55.♘g6 ♗d7 56.♘e7 ♗xb5 57.♘c8 ♗c6 58.♘xb6=;

  C) There is no time for waiting moves: 38...♗e6? 39.♕e8 ♔g7 40.♕e7 ♔g6 41.♕e8 ♔g5 42.♕e7 ♕f6 43.♕h7 ♗f5 44.♕c7=
The most sensible candidate moves were 38...♕e6, 38...h4 and 38...e3.

Viktoriia Kirchei	1663
Davaakhuu Munkhzul	1582

World Youth Chess Championship
Halkidiki 2015 (U10 Girls)

1) **Find sensible candidate moves;**
2) **Choose the strongest one.**

This is a typical position in which, if you don't look for candidate moves, you probably won't find

the winning move. It's natural (and wrong) to give check. Look at the position. Black has some weaknesses, but what can White do with only the queen?

In the game, the temptation to give check was too strong for Russian Viktoriia Kirchei:

23.♕h5+? ♔g8 24.♕e8+
24.♕g6 ♕d2 25.♕xd6 ♗d4 26.♕d8+ ♔h7 27.♕f8 ♕xc2 28.♕f5+ ♔g8 29.♔h2 ♗d3 30.♕c8+ ♔h7 31.♕f5+ ♔g8=

24...♔h7 25.♕f8 ♗h4
Better was 25...♕d2. For example: 26.♕xd6 ♕f4 27.b4 ♕g3 28.bxc5 ♕xc3 29.♖c1 ♕b2 30.♖f1 ♗xf1 31.♕f8 ♗xc5 32.♕f5+ ♔g8 33.♕e6+ ♔f8 34.♕c8+ ♔f7 35.♕e6+ ♔f8=

26.♕xd6 ♗f6
With only a slight advantage for White. Eventually Black won.
Other possibilities:

  A) 23.♕f5+? ♔g8 24.♖b1 ♗g3 25.b4 ♘d3 26.cxd3 ♕xc3 27.♕e6+ ♔h8 28.♕xd6 ♗xd3 29.♕c6 ♕d2 30.♕c8+ ♔h7 31.♕f5+ ♔g8=;

  B) 23.♖d1? ♕e3 24.a4 (24.b4 ♕xc3 25.bxc5 ♗xc5 26.♕e6+ ♔f8 27.♖b1 ♗b6 28.♕xd6+ ♔g8 29.♕e6+ ♔h7 30.d6 ♕xc2 31.♖xb6 ♕c1+ 32.♔h2 ♕f4+=) 24...♗e1 25.♕f5+ ♔g8 26.b4 ♗xc3 27.bxc5 ♕xc5 28.♕e6+ ♔f8 29.♕f5+ ♔e8 30.♕e6+ ♔f8 31.♕f5+ ♔g8 32.♕e6+ ♔h7 33.♕f5+ ♔g8=;

  C) 23.a4? ♔g8 24.♘b5 ♗xb5 25.♕c8+ (25.axb5?! ♕xe4) 25...♔h7 26.♕f5+ ♔g8 27.axb5 ♘xe4 28.♕c8+ ♔h7 29.♕f5+ ♔g8=;

  D) 23.♖b1! The rook enters into play and the black knight is driven away: 23...♔g8 24.b4 ♘b3 (24...♘b7 25.♕c8+ ♔h7 26.b5+–; 24...♘d3 25.♘e2 ♕e3 26.cxd3 h5 27.♕e6+ ♔h7

28.♖f1 ♗xd3 29.♕f5+ ♔h6 30.♕xf2
♕xe2 31.♕xe2 ♗xe2 32.♖f7+–)
25.♖xb3 ♕e3 26.♕d1 ♗c4 27.♖a3
♕f4 28.♖a4 ♕e3 29.♘b1 ♕xe4 30.b5
♕xd5 31.♘c3 ♕f7 32.♘e4 ♗xb5
33.♘xd6 ♕d7 34.♕d5+ ♔h7 35.♕xb5
♕xd6 36.♕d3+ ♕xd3 37.cxd3+–
By reasoning about weaknesses,
it was not so difficult to find
23.♖b1!, since the black knight is
the defender of Black's weak light
squares.

> To find candidate moves, it's often
> a good idea to pay attention to
> every single piece. In this way,
> it will be more difficult to miss
> something.

At the 2016 World Cadets Chess
Championship (Open U8), Azeri
boy Farid Orujov took the bronze
medal.

Farid Orujov   1377
Batsukh Anand   1708

World Cadets Chess Championship
Batumi 2016 (Open U8)

1) **Find sensible candidate moves;**
2) **Choose the strongest one.**

The game continued with

13.♕e3? cxd4 14.cxd4 ♘d5
Better was 14...♘xe5 15.dxe5 ♘e4
16.♕e2 ♕c7.
15.♕g3 ♘xe5 16.dxe5
With unclear play.
Other moves:
  A) 13.♘g6? ♖e8 14.♘xe7+ ♕xe7=;
  B) 13.♗f4? ♘xe5 14.♗xe5 a6
15.dxc5 b5 16.♖ad1 ♕c8 17.♗d3
♕xc5=;
  C) 13.♗b5? ♕c7 14.♗f4 ♗d6
15.♘xd7 ♘xd7 16.♗xd6 ♕xd6
17.♖ad1 ♘f6=;
  D) White had to show some
combinative vision. It was not
difficult to find 13.♘xf7!. For
example: 13...♖xf7 14.♕xe6 (14.♗xe6?
♘f8 15.♗xf7+ ♔xf7) 14...♕e8

analysis diagram

15.♕xe7 ♕xe7 16.♖xe7+–
To improve combinative vision, a
good idea is to learn and practise
tactical patterns, that is, particular
positions that occur in games
and where often a tactical idea is
possible.
Tactical patterns can be divided
into mating patterns (Anastasia's,
Anderssen's, Arabian, Back-rank,
Cozio's, Damiano's, etc.) and other
tactical patterns (double attack,
discovered attack, pinning, X-ray,
etc.).

> Pattern recognition helps to quickly understand the position and to find the best move or the best plan. There are many books and internet training sites that can help with tactics. Pattern training provides guidance in strategic positions as well. An example, which we saw in the first part, is the position with a hook. A hook can permit, for example, a minority attack or an attack against the castled king.

There is a question. Would White have played the right move if he had applied our model for searching candidate moves? It seems he used seven minutes before making his move. Hence, the right move was probably analysed. Perhaps he didn't see that after 13.♘xf7! ♖xf7 14.♕xe6 ♕e8, it was possible to play 15.♕xe7 ♕xe7 16.♖xe7+–, because the ♖f7 is pinned. It is not enough to see the best move, you have to play it! Maybe it was a problem of visualisation, namely the ability to have a correct image of the chessboard and pieces in our mind. How can we improve our chess visualisation? Some exercises can help.

• Ask yourself what colour a random square on the board is. Do the same for diagonals;
• Picture in your head the knight's route from a1 to h8 and play out the moves. Do the same with other routes;
• Follow games without a board, for example, by looking at a game in a chess magazine and playing over the moves in your head;

• Look at the previous diagram in this book for half a minute. Then close the book and put the position on a chessboard;
• With a chessboard, before analysing variations of one game, remember the position of the game. Then analyse variations, moving and exchanging pieces. When you have finished analysing, put the position of the game on the chessboard, rather than replaying the game from the first move;
• Play blindfold games (beginning with simple endgames);
• Last, but not least: solve many tactical exercises.

Returning to our exercise, if you followed the model given at the beginning of this chapter, you probably only calculated 13.♘xf7!. As this move worked, you didn't have to calculate other moves.

Kirill Volotovsky   2021
Jonas Bjerre   2193
European Youth Chess Championship
Porec 2015 (U12 Open)

1) **Find sensible candidate moves;**
2) **Choose the strongest one.**

The position is rather unclear. White is trying to attack on the kingside, while Black seems to be preparing a counterattack in the centre.

After the knight moves, White is a bit better:

A) 17...♘g6 18.h5 ♘e5 19.♗e2 d5 20.h6;

B) 17...♘g2 18.♘f5 exf5 19.♗xg2 fxe4 20.fxe4 ♗c6 21.♕d4 ♕g3 22.♕d2;

C) More interesting is 17...♗f8, preparing 18...d5. For example: 18.h5 d5 19.♗xf4 ♕xf4 20.♕xb7 ♖ab8 21.♕xa6 dxe4 22.♗xb5 ♕g3 23.fxe4 ♖xd1+ 24.♖xd1 ♕xg5, with chances for both sides.

In the game, Black played

17...d5!?

Jonas decided to take the initiative!

18.♗xf4 ♕xf4 19.♕xb7

19...♗c5!

Only move.

A) Before playing 17... d5!?, Black had to see that 19...♕xg3 loses to 20.♕xe7 ♕xf3 21.♗d3 ♖e8 22.♕b4+−;

B) 19...♕xf3 loses to 20.♗e2 ♕xg3 21.♕xe7+−;

Other moves leave White better:

C) 19...♗f8 20.♖h3 ♖ab8 21.♕c6 ♖bc8 22.♕b6 ♗c5 23.♕a5 ♕xf3 24.♖d3 ♕f2 25.♕d2 ♕xd2 26.♖xd2;

D) 19...♗d6 20.exd5 ♕xf3 (20...♕xg3 21.dxe6 fxe6 22.♗d3+−) 21.♗e2 ♕xg3 22.♖hf1 exd5 23.♕xf7+ ♔h8 24.♗d3 ♕xh4 25.♗xh7 ♖f8 26.♕xd5 ♖xf1 27.♕xa8+ ♗f8 28.♕xa6 ♔xh7 29.♕xd6+−

20.♘e2

A) 20.exd5 ♕xg3=;

B) 20.♖h3 ♖db8 21.♕c6 ♖c8 22.♕d7 ♖d8 23.♕b7 ♖db8=;

C) 20.♘h5 ♕xf3 21.♗d3 dxe4 22.♖hf1 ♕xh5 23.♕xe4 ♖ac8=

20...♕d6

The white queen risks being trapped.

21.♘d4?!

21.e5 ♕xe5 22.b4 ♗f2 23.g6 hxg6 24.♕e7 ♗e3 is unclear.

21...♗xd4 22.♖xd4

22.exd5 ♕b4 23.c3 ♗xc3 24.♖h2 ♗e5 25.a3 ♕a4 26.♖hd2 exd5, and Black is better.

22...♖db8

22...♕c5! 23.c3 ♖a7 24.♕xa7 ♕xa7

23.♖xd5 ♕g3 24.♕d7 exd5 25.♗d3 ♖d8 26.♕f5 g6 27.♕f6 ♖d6 28.♕e7 dxe4 29.♗xe4?!

Better was 29.fxe4 ♖c8 30.a3, and White is worse, but can fight on.

29...♕xh4 30.♖c1 ♖ad8

And Black won.

The most sensible candidate moves were 17...♗f8 and 17...d5. One was quiet, preparing the pawn push, while the other was more direct. If you found only one of these moves, this shows what you are good at and what you need to improve.

CHAPTER 7

Attack

A famous chess aphorism is 'The threat is stronger than the execution.' It could give the wrong idea that the threat is really better than the execution. Of course, the meaning of the aphorism is different, as explained by Eugene Znosko-Borovsky in his book *The Middle Game in Chess*: 'It is a perfectly true saying that a threat is often stronger than its execution. An insignificant threat which persists for a certain length of time and burdens our play, forces us to bear it in mind, and to try to guess at what precise moment the enemy will choose to set it in motion. It is useless to insist that the threat is not serious, that it is a sham: circumstances may change, and very suddenly the same threat becomes acute and most embarrassing.' He uses the example of the Ruy Lopez. After 1.e4 e5 2.♘f3 ♘c6 3.♗b5, the ♙e5 is not really attacked, 'but here again it may happen that a moment's inattention in the course of operations will cost us the ♙e5, or at least cause us much trouble in winning it back.'

We can therefore say that a serious and not prevented threat must be executed.

This chapter is mainly devoted to the execution of threats, namely the final phase of an attack or the sudden effect of a blunder.

Are you a good executor? Test yourself!

Magdalena Harazinska   1761
Xue Bai   1639
World Youth Chess Championship
Halkidiki 2015 (U12 Girls)

___

1.d4 d5 2.c4 e6 3.♘f3 ♘f6 4.g3 ♗e7 5.♗g2 0-0 6.cxd5 exd5 7.♕c2 ♘c6 8.a3 ♖e8 9.0-0 ♗f8 10.♗g5 h6 11.♗xf6 ♕xf6 12.♘c3 ♗e6 13.e3 ♖ad8 14.b4 a6 15.♘a4 ♗f5 16.♕c3 ♕e6 17.♖fc1 ♖c8
A little better was 17...♕c8 18.♘c5 ♘b8.
18.♘c5 ♗xc5 19.♕xc5
The attack against the king is the most dangerous kind of attack, and has been given the greatest attention by chess players and chess writers, but it is not the only way to attack. If you play 1.d4 with white, you'll often attack on the queenside, where usually Black's king will not be castled.

19...♗d3

More precise was 19...♗e4 20.♘d2 ♗xg2.

20.♘d2 ♘e7 21.♕c3 ♗g6

Again, it was better to play 21...♗e4. For example: 22.♗f1 c6, with a small plus for White.

22.♘b3 b6?!

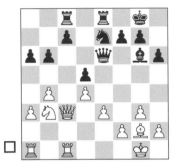

How should White continue?

23.♗f1!

Attacking the weakness. Black shouldn't have weakened the light squares, preferring 22...♕b6, and if 23.a4, then 23...c6.

23...b5 24.♘c5 ♕b6 25.a4 c6 26.axb5

Better was 26.♖a3 ♖cd8 27.♖ca1, exchanging pawns and penetrating with the rook at the right moment.

26...axb5 27.♖a6 ♕b8 28.♖ca1 ♗f5 29.♖1a3 h5 30.♕a1

Magdalena was in a fighting mood that day. She applied the famous 'Alekhine's gun', namely the

formation with the queen behind the rooks. It was so named after the game Alekhine-Nimzowitsch, San Remo 1930. It is used, as in this game, for penetrating into a rook's file (usually exchanging pawns only after having prepared the 'gun'), but also to battle against a central isolated pawn.

30...h4 31.♖a7 hxg3 32.hxg3 ♕d6 33.♖3a6 ♖b8 34.♕a5 ♕h6

35.♖c7?!

A little better was 35.♖a8 ♖xa8 36.♖xa8 ♖xa8 37.♕xa8+ ♔h7 38.♕e8 ♕f6 39.♗d3, with a slight advantage for White. Now, Black organizes dangerous counterplay.

35...♕h5 36.♕a1 ♖bc8 37.♖aa7 ♖xc7 38.♖xc7 g5! 39.♗g2 ♔g7

Now, it is Xue who is in a fighting mood, and White must defend.

40.f3?

The game could end peacefully in a nice way: 40.♘d7 ♗h3 41.♘e5 ♗xg2

42.♔xg2 ♖h8 43.♖xe7 ♕h3+ 44.♔f3
♕f5+ 45.♔e2 ♕c2+ 46.♔f3 ♕e4+
40...♗h3

41.g4?
White had to try 41.♕b2 ♘f5
42.♗xh3 (not 42.g4? ♕h4 43.gxf5
♕e1+ 44.♔h2 ♗xf5; 42.e4 ♘xg3
43.♖xc6 ♗xg2 44.♕xg2 ♕h4
45.♖a6 dxe4 46.fxe4 ♘xe4)
42...♕xh3 43.♕g2, eventually
entering into an inferior endgame
after 43...♕xg2+ 44.♔xg2 ♖xe3
45.♖xc6 g4 46.fxg4 ♖xg3+ 47.♔f2
♖xg4.
41...♕h4 42.♖a7 ♗xg2 43.♔xg2

How should Black conclude the attack?

You see here the difference between weaknesses on the queenside and on the kingside. The first ones rarely lead to a short-term defeat, while weaknesses on the kingside can provoke an immediate defeat.

Now, a correct calculation could decide the game.
43...♖h8?
Black could only win with tactical play:
   A) 43...♘g6! 44.♕g1 ♘f4+! 45.♔f1
♘h3 46.♕g2 ♖xe3–+;
   B) Also good was 43...♘f5!? 44.gxf5
♖xe3, with the threat 45... ♖e1:
45.♘e6+ ♔h6 (45...♔f6?? 46.♖xf7+!
♔xf7 47.♕a7+ ♔e8 48.♕b8+ ♔e7
49.♕f8+ ♔d7 50.♕d8#) 46.♕f1 g4!
(46...♖e1? 47.♖xf7! ♖xf1 48.♖f6+
♔h7 49.♖f7+ ♔g8 50.♖f8+ ♔h7=)
47.♘f4 gxf3+ 48.♖xf3 ♕g5+ 49.♔f2
♖xf3+ 50.♔xf3 ♕xf5–+
44.♕g1
Now, everything is well-defended.
**44...♘g6 45.♘d3 ♕h3+ 46.♔f2 ♖e8
47.♖a1 ♖e7 48.♕h1 ♕xh1 49.♖xh1
♖a7 50.♖b1 ♖a3 51.♔e2 f6 52.♖b2
♘h4 53.f4?!**
53.♖c2 ♘g2 54.♖d2 ♔g6=
53...♘g2?!
53...f5! 54.fxg5 fxg4 55.♖c2 g3, and
Black is better.
**54.fxg5 fxg5 55.♖c2 ♔h7 56.♔d2
♔g7 57.♔e2 ♔f8 58.♔d2 ♔e7
59.♔e2 ♔e8 60.♔d2 ♔e7 61.♔e2
♔f8 62.♔d2 ♔g7 63.♔e2**
Threefold repetition, but play continued.
**63...♖xd3 64.♔xd3 ♘e1+ 65.♔d2
♘xc2 66.♔xc2 ♔g6 67.♔c3 ♔f6
68.♔d2 ♔e7 69.♔c3 ♔d6 ½-½**

Some general suggestions about attack are given in chess books. The three most often-repeated are probably:
 1) Bring all your pieces into the attack;
 2) Open lines for your pieces (mainly for the rooks);

3) Weaken the opponent's defence (mainly his pawn structure).

We saw in the last diagram that Black had a winning combination by including all the pieces in the attack. She had already opened files for the rook and weakened important squares in White's defence. I wish to stress that the first suggestion has several exceptions. For example, sometimes the attack is possible only with two or three pieces, and the attacker can lose important tempi bringing other pieces into the attack.

Yanbin Wang
Ariel Erenberg   2366

World Youth Chess Championship
Halkidiki 2015 (U14 Open)

1.c4 c5 2.♘c3 ♘c6 3.g3 g6 4.♗g2 ♗g7 5.♘f3 d6 6.0-0 e6 7.a3 ♘ge7 8.♖b1 a5 9.d3 0-0 10.♗g5 h6 11.♗d2 g5 12.h4 g4 13.♘e1 f5 14.♘c2 e5 15.b4 axb4 16.axb4 f4 17.♘d5 ♖a2 18.b5 ♘d4 19.♘xd4 cxd4 20.♗e1 ♔h8 21.♘b4 ♖a8 22.♗e4 ♘f5 23.♘d5 ♗e6 24.♖a1 ♖xa1 25.♕xa1 ♘xh4! 26.♕a5
26.gxh4? f3!–+
26...♕g5

We have reached a complicated position. White attacks Black's weak pawns on the queenside, but Black's attack on the kingside is much more dangerous.
27.♕c7 ♗xd5 28.gxh4
  A) 28.♗xd5? f3 29.exf3 ♘xf3+ 30.♗xf3 (30.♔g2 ♕h5 31.♖h1 ♕f5 32.♗xf3 ♕xf3+ 33.♔g1 ♕xd3–+) 30...gxf3 31.♕d7 ♕h5 32.c5 ♔h7 33.♗a5 ♖f5–+;
  B) 28.cxd5 fxg3 29.fxg3 ♕e3+ 30.♗f2 ♕xe2 31.♕xd6 ♘f3+ 32.♗xf3 ♕xf3 33.♕g6 ♕xd5 34.♕xg4 ♕xb5, and Black is better.
28...♕xh4 29.cxd5 f3 30.♕xd6 fxe2 31.♕g6

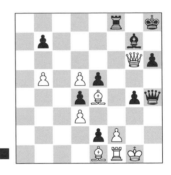

How should Black proceed with the attack?

31...♕g3+!
The only move to fight for an advantage. After 31...exf1♕+ 32.♔xf1 ♔g8 33.♕h7+ ♔f7 34.♗b4 ♖a8 (34...♕f6 35.♗xf8 ♔xf8 36.♘e2 b6 37.♗f5) 35.♕g6+ ♔g8 36.d6, White is slightly better. Black must remove the white bishop from the e4-h7 diagonal.
32.♗g2 exf1♕+ 33.♔xf1 ♖f6 34.♕e8+ ♗f8

35.d6?

After 35.♗e4 ♕f4 36.d6 ♖xd6
37.♗xb7 ♕f6 38.♕h5 g3 39.f3, Black
is better, but perhaps not winning.
**35...♕xd3+ 36.♔g1 ♕e2 37.d7
♕xe1+ 38.♔h2 ♕xf2 39.d8♕**
39.♕xe5 ♕h4+ 40.♔g1 ♗e7–+

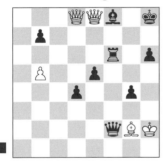

How should Black continue?

39...g3+?

It's not easy to play in terrible time
trouble with an opponent who has
two queens! Here, Black had two
good solutions:
  A) Most simple was 39...♕f4+
40.♔h1 g3 (or 40...♕c1+ 41.♔h2
♕f4+, and Black has passed the
time control) 41.♕c8 (41.♕xf6+
♕xf6 42.♕h5 e4) 41...♖f5–+;
  B) Or 39...♖f5 40.♕d5 (40.♕g6
♕f4+ 41.♔g1 g3 42.♕xf5 ♕xf5
43.♕a5 d3–+) 40...♕f4+ 41.♔g1 g3
42.♕f3 ♕c1+ 43.♕f1 (43.♗f1 ♖xf3
44.♕xe5+ ♔g8 45.♕e6+ ♖f7–+)

43...♕e3+ 44.♔h1 ♖xf1+ 45.♗xf1
♕f3+ 46.♔g2 ♕d1+ 47.♔f1 ♕xf1#.
40.♔h3 ♕f5+ 41.♔xg3 d3
With other moves, Black has only
perpetual check. For example:
41...♖g6+ 42.♔h2 ♕h5+ 43.♔g1
♕d1+ 44.♔h2

42.♕ee7?!
This inaccuracy doesn't change the
result.
  A) Better is 42.♔h2 ♕f4+ 43.♔h3
d2 44.♕h5 ♖d6 45.♕xe5+ ♕xe5
46.♕xf8+ ♔h7 47.♕f7+ ♔h8
48.♕f8+ ♔h7=;
  B) Or 42.♕dd7 ♕f4+ 43.♔h3
♕e3+ 44.♔h2 ♕f4+ 45.♔h3=.
**42...♕g5+ 43.♔h2 ♕h4+ 44.♔g1
♖f1+ 45.♔xf1 ♕xe7 46.♕xe7 ♗xe7
47.♗xb7 ♔g7 48.♗e4 d2 49.♔e2
♔f6 50.♔xd2 ♔g5 51.♔e3 ♔g4
52.♔f2 h5 53.♔g2 ♗c5 54.♗c6 h4
55.♗d7+ ♔g5 56.♔f3 ♗b6 57.♔e4
♔f6 58.♔f3 ♔e7 59.♗c6 ♔d6
60.♔g4 ♗d8 61.♔h3 ♔c5 62.♔h2
♗a5 63.♔h3 ♗e1 64.♔h2 ♗f2
65.♔g2 ♗g3 66.♔h3 ♔d4 67.b6 e4
68.♗xe4 ♔xe4 69.b7 ½-½**

In the last two games the player
with the advantage had two
winning moves, but chose only a
drawing move. In the last game,
probably if Black (with only one
minute left) had remained calm, he

would have seen that after 39...♛f4+ 40.♚h1 ♛c1+, he could pass the time control. The situation was different in the other game, and Black had to find one of the two tactical ideas.

> When solving chess exercises, always give yourself a limited amount of time. This helps you to stay focused and to make good decisions in time trouble.

Haik Martirosyan	2391
Alejandro Perez Garcia	2165

European Youth Chess Championship
Prague 2016 (U14 Open)

1.♘f3 ♘f6 2.c4 c6 3.♘c3 d5 4.e3 ♘bd7 5.♕c2 e5 6.cxd5 ♘xd5 7.♗e2 ♘xc3 8.bxc3 ♗d6 9.d4 ♕e7 10.♖b1 0-0 11.0-0 ♖e8 12.♖e1 ♘f6
Better is 12...e4 13.♘d2 ♗c7.
13.c4
13.dxe5 ♗xe5 14.♘xe5 ♕xe5 15.♗d3, with a small plus for White.

13...e4
With this move, Black closes the centre and begins an attack on the kingside. White must act quickly on the queenside.
14.♘d2 ♘g4 15.♗xg4 ♗xg4 16.♘f1 b6 17.♗b2 ♕g5 18.c5 bxc5 19.♗a3 ♖e6 20.♗xc5

How should Black continue?

The game continued with
20...♗xh2+!
20...♗f3? 21.♘g3
21.♘xh2
21.♚xh2 ♗f3! 22.♘g3 ♖h6+ 23.♚g1 ♕h4–+
21...♗f3 22.g3
22.g4 ♖h6
22...♕h5 23.♘xf3 exf3 24.♕b3 ♕h3 25.♕b8+ ♖e8 0-1

White had to play 15.g3, and afterwards not permit the sacrifice by playing 20.♘g3 (20.dxc5? ♗xh2+ 21.♘xh2 ♗f3–+). After 20...♗xg3 21.fxg3 cxd4 22.exd4 e3, Black is better, but the position is complicated.
Black played a nice game. All his pieces were well-placed and ready for the 'execution'. As in the previous game, Black exploited the weaknesses of the light squares f3-g2-h3.

The next game was played in the 11th and final round of the 2015 World Youth Chess Championship (U12 Girls). The USA representative Yip was second with 8.5/10 points (first was Bulgarian Salimova with 9.0), Bach was 4th-6th with 7.5.

Carissa Yip   2007
Ngoc Thuy Duong Bach   1707

World Youth Chess Championship
Halkidiki 2015 (U12 Girls)

The girls were in terrible time trouble, and had another dozen moves to play before the time control.

How should Black continue? Give yourself only one minute to solve the puzzle.

26...♖af8?

A) Black could win with 26...♖f3! 27.♗xf3 (27.♕e2 ♖xa3) 27...♕xh3+ 28.♔g1 ♘xf3+ 29.♔f2 ♗d4! 30.♖g1+ ♘xg1 (30...♔h8−+) 31.♕xd4 ♕h2+ 32.♔f1 ♖f8+ 33.♔e1 ♕e2#;

B) 26...♖d8 27.♖f1 ♖xf1+ 28.♗xf1 ♖f8 29.♕g1 ♕e4+ 30.♗g2 ♕g6 31.♕e1 leaves White better, as does;

C) 26...♘f7 27.♖b4 ♕f6 28.♖g4 ♔h8 29.♗b4

27.♗xd6 ♖8f3 28.♖xg7+! ♔xg7

29.♗xe5+?

29.♕xe5+ ♔h7 (29...♔g6 30.♖g1 ♔h7 31.♕e7++−) 30.♕e7+ ♕xe7 31.♗xe7+−

29...♔f7?

29...♔h7 30.♕e1 ♖xh3+ 31.♔g1 ♖xg2+ 32.♔xg2 ♕g4+ 33.♗g3 ♖xg3+ 34.♕xg3 ♕e4+ 35.♕f3 ♕xb1 gave Black drawing chances.

30.♗xf3?

30.♕xf3+ ♖xf3 31.♗xf3 ♕xh3+ 32.♔g1 ♕xf3 33.♖f1+−

30...♕xh3+ 31.♔g1

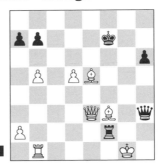

How should Black continue? Give yourself only one minute to solve the puzzle.

31...♖xf3?

The last mistake. Much better was 31...♖g2+! 32.♗xg2 ♕xe3+ 33.♔h1 ♕xe5, with advantage to Black.

32.♕e2

This wins, but 32.♕xf3+! ♕xf3 33.♖f1 was simpler.

32...♕f5 33.♖f1 ♕g4+ 34.♕g2 ♖xf1+ 35.♔xf1 ♕d1+ 36.♔f2 ♕d2+ 37.♔g1 ♕b4 38.♕g7+ ♔e8 39.♕g8+ ♔e7 40.♕e6+ 1-0

Salimova only drew, but took the gold medal on tiebreak, ahead of Yip.

Motahare Asadi   1980
Judit Juhasz   1896
World Cadets Chess Championship
Batumi 2016 (U12 Girls)

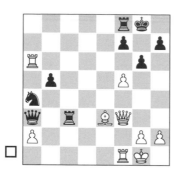

How can White start a vicious attack against the black king?

27.fxg6 hxg6
27...罩xe3? 28.gxf7+ 罩xf7 29.豐xf7+
28.豐d5!!
Motahare used ten minutes to play 27.fxg6 and only a few seconds for this move. Everything had been well-calculated. Not 28.罩xg6+? fxg6 29.豐d5+ 含g7 30.皇d4+ 含h6 31.罩xf8 豐xf8 32.皇xc3 包xc3 33.豐d2+ g5 34.豐xc3 豐d6, with a probable draw.
28...罩c6
28...罩xe3? 29.罩xg6+ 含h7 30.豐h5#
29.罩xc6 豐xe3+ 30.含h1 含g7
31.罩c7 豐e8 32.h3!

32...含g8

32...b4 33.豐d4+ 含g8 34.罩f6 含h7
35.罩f4 含g8 36.罩h4+−
33.罩f6! 含g7 34.罩e6 豐d8

35.罩d7
35.罩xf7+ 含xf7 36.罩d6+ 含g7
37.罩xd8
**35...豐c8 36.豐d4+ 含h7 37.罩ee7
豐c1+ 38.含h2 豐f1 39.罩e4 1-0**

A great game by the Iranian girl, who finished the tournament in fourth place.

Viktor Gazik   2431
Shant Sargsyan   2357
World Youth Chess Championship
Halkidiki 2015 (U14 Open)

How can White continue the attack?

25.e5!
After 25.h4 罩f7 26.hxg5 包e5 27.gxf6 含h8, Black is worse, but can fight

on. Of course, not 25.♘xf8? ♖xf8, and the black knight will be very strong on e5.
25...♘xe5
25....dxe5 26.♗xc6
26.♘xf8 ♖xf8 27.♗d5+ ♖f7 28.♕xf6 ♗b7 29.♕xg5+ ♔f8 30.♗xf7 ♘xf7 31.♕g3
And White won.

This was a last-round game, with the Slovak finishing 3rd-4th (fourth on tiebreak).

Valery Skatchkov   2104
Vincent Keymer   2402
World Cadets Chess Championship
Batumi 2016 (U12 Open)

1) **Is 19...♕h4 the best move or is Black in trouble after 20.h3 ?**
2) **Can you suggest another move?**

19...♕h4!
Other moves are inferior.
   A) Of course, not 19...♘gxe5? 20.f4+−;
   B) 19...♕g5 20.cxd5 cxd5 (20...♕h4 21.h3 ♘xf2 22.♔xf2 ♘g5 23.♕e1 ♘e4+ 24.♔f3 ♘xg3 25.♕xg3 ♕e4+ 26.♔f2 ♕c2+ 27.♔g1 ♕xb2 28.d6 gives a small advantage to White) 21.♕d4 is nearly equal.

20.h3 ♘xf2!
20...♘gxe5 21.♖ad1 is unclear.
21.♔xf2 ♘g5 22.♕e1 ♘e4+
22...f4 23.exf4 ♘e4+ 24.♔g1 ♕xg3 gives Black only a small plus.
23.♔f3 ♘xg3

24.♗c1?
After 24.♕xg3 ♕e4+ 25.♔f2 ♕c2+ 26.♔g1 ♕xb2, Black is clearly better, but at least White can play on.
24...♕e4+ 25.♔xg3 ♕xe5+ 0-1

Bartosz Fiszer   2009
Jan Klimkowski   1761
European Youth Chess Championship
Mamaia 2017 (U10 Open)

How can Black continue his attack?

25...d5!
Opening lines.
25...♖ad8?! 26.h3 ♗c8∓
26.fxe5?

A) 26.exd5 ♗f5 27.♕e2 exf4∓;

B) 26.c3 ♗b6∓

26...♕xe5 27.c3 ♗b6 28.♕xd5

28.♗c6 ♖ad8 (28...dxe4 29.♕d5 ♕c7 30.♗xa8 ♗f3 31.♕c6 ♕d8 32.♕d5 ♕c8−+) 29.♗xd5 ♗e6 30.c4 f5−+

Now, Black has a rather surprising and very strong move. Do you see it?

28...♕xd5?

A) Unfortunately for him and for the correctness of this game, Black didn't play 28...♕e6!! 29.♗c4 (after 29.♕xe6 fxe6+30.♔e1 ♖ad8, White must give up the bishop and will be mated after a few moves; another sad possibility for White was 29.♗f4 ♖ad8 30.♕c6 ♗h3 31.♔e1 ♕g4−+) 29...♖ad8 30.♕xe6 fxe6+, and White gets mated by force in a few moves, for example: 31.♔g2 ♗f2 32.♔g3 ♖df8 33.h3 ♖8f3 34.♔h4 ♖h2 35.♖xh2 ♗f2 36.♖xf2 ♖xh3#;

B) Another chance was to avoid exchanging the queens with 28...♕e7?!, and after 29.♗f4 ♖ad8 30.♕c6 ♗d7 31.♕xb6 ♕xe4 32.♔g1 ♕xf4 33.♕f2 ♕xg5, Black is clearly better, but must work hard to win the game.

29.exd5 ♗f3 30.♖g1 ♗xg1 31.♔xg1 ♗xd5 32.c4 ♗e4 33.♗d2 ♖fc8 34.♖c1 ♗c6 35.♗e3 ♖ab8 36.♗f4 ♖a8 37.♗e3 ♖ab8 38.♗f4 ♖a8 39.♗e3 ♖ab8 ½-½

CHAPTER 8

Defence

We all train ourselves a lot to attack, but much less to defend. As we'll see, often the youngsters were unable to withstand their opponent's attack. How can we react correctly to an attack? It all begins with a correct evaluation of the position. Ask yourself questions, such as: 'does my position have or can it have weaknesses that can be exploited by my opponent?' and 'how are my pieces and those of my opponent placed?'

If everything is under control, the attack will be withstood without any particular effort. Otherwise, it will be necessary to act in some way, for example, by bringing another piece into the defence.

A list of suggestions for the defender:

1) Identify all the threats;

2) Remember to search for candidate moves. When looking for them, consider all your pieces, beginning with the king;

3) If you see a good move immediately and you have some time, wait for a moment! Pay attention, especially if the good move is a capture. Captures have the power to override every other thought, including much better moves;

4) Avoid unforced passive moves! When we are defending, it often happens that we make unforced passive moves. Our opponent presses, and it becomes natural for us to defend. We must be sure that there is not something better, such as a counterattack. In other words, always consider not only our weaknesses, but also those of our opponent;

5) Don't be overactive! When under pressure, sometimes we only need to defend our passive, but healthy position. If we lose objectivity, we can try to counterattack, creating other weaknesses in our own camp;

6) Don't panic! Overactivity, for example, can be provoked by panic. If this happens, take a deep breath and dedicate yourself to completing the first two points on this list;

7) In some positions, it's easier to eliminate losing moves than to find the saving one (if it exists, of course!). Hence, play the move that remains after seeing that other moves are losing (method of elimination);

8) Remember that prevention is better than the cure! Make good use of prophylactic thinking. If possible, trade the attacker's strongest pieces.

In this chapter, we'll examine critical positions, where a defensive move can decide the game.

Ariel Erenberg   2366
Artur Davtyan   2144

World Youth Chess Championship
Halkidiki 2015 (U14 Open)

White threatens h2-h4-h5. How can Black defend?

The position is complicated, and although White's threat is clear, it's unclear how to prevent it.

A) The game continued with 39...♖cc7? 40.h4 ♖xc4 41.h5 ♖c1+ 42.♔h2 ♖d7 43.♕xg6#;

B) 39...♖xc4? 40.h4+− was not much better;

C) Nor was 39...♖xd5? 40.♖xd5 ♕c7 41.h4 e3 42.♘xf6+ (42.♘xe3 ♖xe3 43.h5 ♖e1+ 44.♔h2 ♕h8 45.hxg6) 42...gxf6 43.h5 exf2+ 44.♔xf2 ♔g8 45.♕xg6+ ♖g7 46.♕d3+−.

Black didn't deal with the threat. There was a way to continue the battle:

39...♕c7!

If White now plays 40.h4?, Black is better after 40...♕xd8! 41.♖xc5 bxc5 42.h5 ♕e8.

40.♖xc5

Better than 40.♖8d7 ♕xd7 41.♕xd7 ♖xd7 42.♖xd7 ♔g8 43.♖xa7 ♖xc4, with good chances to draw, for example: 44.♘e3 (44.♖a6 ♖c3 45.a4 ♖a3 46.♖xb6 ♖xa4 47.♖b8+ ♔f7

48.♖b7+ ♘e7) 44...♖c1+ 45.♔g2 ♘e5 46.♘f5 g6 47.♘xh6+ ♔f8 48.h4 f5

40...♕xd8 41.♖d5 ♕g8 42.a4 ♕e6 43.♕xe6 ♖xe6 44.c5 bxc5 45.♖xc5 a6 46.♔f1 axb5 47.axb5 ♖d6

White's position is better, but Black has drawing chances.

Joanna Swiech   1613
Maria Palma   1987

European Youth Chess Championship
Porec 2015 (U14 Girls)

How can Black deal with White's kingside attack?

28...g5?

Other possibilities:

A) 28...♖ee7? 29.♕xg6 ♕xf3 30.gxf3 ♖g7 31.♖xh7+ ♖xh7 32.♕f6+ ♖eg7+ 33.♔h1 ♖h3 34.♕d8+ ♖g8 35.♕xd4+ ♖g7 36.♕d8+ ♖g8 37.♕f6+ ♖g7 38.♗e2+−;

B) 28...♕e6?! 29.♖xf7 ♕xf7 30.♖f4 ♕e7 31.♗c4 ♕g7 32.♕xg7+ ♔xg7 33.♖xd4+−;

C) 28...♖g7?! 29.♖hf4 ♖eg8 30.♗c4 ♕c5 31.♖f2 ♖e8 32.h3 ♖e1+ 33.♔f1 ♔g8 34.♕h4+−;

D) 28...♖e1+! 29.♔f2 (29.♗f1? d3! 30.cxd3 ♖xf1+ 31.♔xf1 ♕xd3+ 32.♔g1 ♗xf3 33.gxf3 ♕xf3−+) 29...♖e8! (or 29...♖ee7!, but not 29...♖xf3+? 30.gxf3+−) 30.♗e4

(30.♖e4 ♖xe4 31.♗xe4 ♕xe4
32.♖xf7 ♕g2+ 33.♔e1=; 30.♖hf4
♕e5 31.♔g1 ♖e1+ 32.♗f1 ♕xd2
33.♖xf7 ♕xh6 34.♖h3 ♕e3+
35.♖xe3 dxe3 is slightly better for
Black; 30.♔g1 ♖e1+=) 30...♖xe4
31.♖xe4 ♕xe4 32.♖xf7 ♕xg2+
33.♔e1 ♕e4+ 34.♔f2 ♕g2+ 35.♔e1=
29.♖h5?
29.♕g6! ♖e1+ (29...gxh4 30.♕xf7+–)
30.♔f2 gxh4 31.♖xf7 ♕xf7 32.♖xf7
♖d1 33.♖xh7+ ♔g8 34.♖xh4 ♖xd2+
35.♔g3 ♖xg2+ 36.♔f4+–
29...♖e1+ 30.♗f1
30.♔f2 ♖ee7 31.♔g1 ♖xf3 32.♕xh7+
♖xh7 33.♖xh7+ ♔g8 34.♗c4 ♔xh7
35.♗xd5 ♖f5–+

How can Black attack?

30...♖xf1+!
Or 30...d3! 31.cxd3 ♕d4+ 32.♔h1
♖xf1++–.
31.♔xf1

31...♖xf3+?

Black could easily win with 31...
d3! 32.cxd3 (32.c4 ♖xf3+ 33.gxf3
♕xf3++–) 32...♕xd3+ 33.♔e1 ♗xf3
34.gxf3 ♕xf3–+. Perhaps Maria was
in time trouble.

> We have to recheck our
> calculations after every move,
> looking for possible improvements
> by both sides.

**32.gxf3 ♕xf3+ 33.♔e1 ♕h1+
34.♔f2 ♕g2+ 35.♔e1 ♕e4+ 36.♔d1
♕h1+ 37.♔e2 ♕e4+ 38.♔d1 ♕h1+
39.♔e2 ♕e4+ 40.♔d1 ½-½**

Islombek Sindarov   2229
Dias Alimbetov   1818
World Cadets Chess Championship
Batumi 2016 (U10 Open)

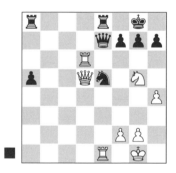

White threatens 32.♖xe5 ♕xe5
33.♕xf7+ ♔h8 34.♕h5 ♕e1+
35.♔h2 ♕b1 36.♘f7+ ♔g8 37.♕d5
h6 38.♘xh6+ ♔h7 39.♕h5, with a
dangerous attack.

How should Black defend?

A) The game went 31...h6??
32.♖xe5! ♕xe5 33.♕xf7+ ♔h8
34.♖xh6+ 1-0;

B) Another possibility was 31...♕c7? 32.♖xe5 ♕c1+ 33.♔h2 ♕f4+ 34.g3 ♕xf2+ 35.♔h3 ♕f1+ 36.♔g4, with a clear advantage to White. For example: 36...♖ab8 37.♔h5! ♖xe5 (37...h6 38.♖xe8+ ♖xe8 39.♕e4 ♕b5 40.♕h7+ ♔f8 41.♖xh6+–) 38.♕xe5 h6 39.♖d7 hxg5 40.♕xb8+ ♔h7 41.♕e5+–
31...a4!

We can see that taking the knight, only gives a draw now: 32.♖xe5 (32.f4? ♕a7+ 33.♔h1 ♘g4–+) 32...♕xe5 33.♕xf7+ ♔h8 34.♖h6 (34.♕h5 ♕e1+ 35.♔h2 ♕b1 36.♘f7+ ♔g8 37.♕d5 ♕b3! – the difference – 38.♘h6+ ♔h8 39.♘f7+ ♔g8=) 34...♕e1+ 35.♔h2 ♕b1 36.♖xh7 (36.f4 gxh6 37.♕f6+ ♔g8 38.♘f7 ♕g6 39.♘xh6+ ♕xh6 40.♕xh6 a3 41.♕g5+ ♔f7 42.♕f5+ ♔g8= or 42...♔e7 43.♕xh7+ ♔d6=) 36...♕xh7 37.♘xh7 ♔xh7 38.♕h5+ ♔g8 39.♕d5+ ♔h7 40.♕f5+ ♔g8=
32.g3 a3 33.♔g2
33.♖xe5 ♕xe5 34.♕xf7+ ♔h8 35.♖h6 ♕e1+ (35...♕g5?? 36.hxg5 gxh6 37.gxh6+–) 36.♔g2 ♕b1 37.♖xh7+ ♕xh7 38.♘xh7 ♔xh7 39.♕h5+ ♔g8 40.♕d5+ ♔h7 with equality.
33...a2 34.♖xe5 ♕xe5 35.♕xf7+ ♔h8 36.♖h6

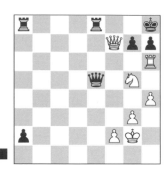

How should Black continue?

36...♕xg5!
Now, the ♙a2 saves the game.
37.hxg5 gxh6 38.g6!
38.gxh6? loses, because of 38... a1♕–+.
38...hxg6 39.♕f6+ ♔g8 40.♕xg6+ ♔h8 41.♕xh6+ ♔g8=

| **Duc Tri Ngo** | 1947 |
| **Kazybek Nogerbek** | 2162 |

World Cadets Chess Championship
Batumi 2016 (U12 Open)

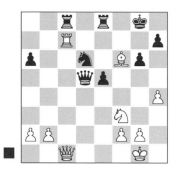

How should Black proceed in this tense situation?

30...♖xc7?
   A) 30...♕b7? 31.♕c4+ ♘xc4 32.♖xb7 ♖c6 33.♗g5 e4 34.♘h2 ♖b6 35.♖a7 h5 36.♘f1 ♖xb2 37.♖xa6 Black is better, but White has drawing chances;

B) 30...♕f7! 31.♖xc8 ♖xc8 32.♕g5
♘e4–+
**31.♕xc7 ♘f7 32.♘xe5 ♕e6 33.♘d7
♕d6 34.♕xd6 ♘xd6 35.♗e5 ♘e4
36.♘f6+ ♘xf6 37.♗xf6**
With a level endgame.

Daniil Maneluk   1991
Richard Stalmach   1735
European Youth Chess Championship
Prague 2016 (U10 Open)

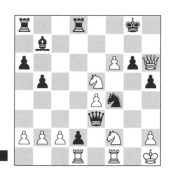

**How does Black deal best with
the mate threats?**

32...♗xe4+?
With this move, Black only has an
even game. Much better is 32...♖d7!
33.h4 ♗xe4+ 34.♔h2 ♖aa7 35.♘xd7
(35.c4 ♗f5 36.♘xd7 ♖xd7–+)
35...♖xd7 36.♕g5 ♗xc2–+.
33.♘xe4 ♕xe4+

How should White defend?

34.♘f3?
After 34.♖f3!, Black has nothing
better than a perpetual check
with 34...♕e1+ 35.♖f1 ♕e4+
36.♖f3=.

**Again, how does Black deal best
with the mating threat?**

34...♘e6?
After 34...♖a7! (34...♖d7? 35.♖xd2!
♖h7 36.♕g5 gives an advantage to
White), Black is better. For example:
35.♕g5 ♖d5 36.♕g3 ♖ad7
35.h3
35.♔g1 ♖d7=
35...♖ac8 36.♔g1 ♕f4??
36...♕f5 37.♖xd2 ♖xd2 38.♘xd2
♕g5+ 39.♕xg5 ♘xg5 40.f7+ ♘xf7
41.c3=
37.♕xg6+ ♔f8

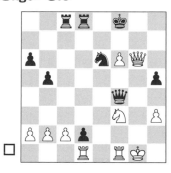

**How does White improve his
position?**

38.f7?

The best solution was 38.♖f2! (other
moves, such as 38.♔h1 or 38.c3,
probably win, but much less clearly)
38...♕e3 39.♕xh5 ♖c7 40.♔f1 ♖dd7
41.♖g2.

38...♕e3+?

After 38...♔e7, White is only a little
better in a complicated position.

39.♔h1 ♘f4? 40.♘g5??

White could win in many ways,
but best was 40.♕g8+ ♔e7 41.♕g7
♔e6 42.f8♕ ♖xf8 43.♖xd2 ♖cd8
44.♕h6+ ♖f6 45.♖xd8 ♖xh6
46.♖e8+ ♔d5 47.♖xe3+−.

40...♘xg6 0-1

Tagir Salemgareev	2083
Semen Lomasov	2357

European Youth Chess Championship
Porec 2015 (U14 Open)

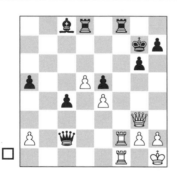

What should White play?

After examining the position,
it's clear that White has a great
material disadvantage without
having any winning attacking
chances. Therefore, he should play
for a draw: 34.♕h4! ♖xf2 35.♕e7+
♔h6 (35...♔g8 36.♕xd8+ ♔g7
37.♕e7+ ♔g8=) 36.♕h4+ ♔g7=

34.♕xe5+?!

**Where would you put your king,
to defend this position with
black?**

34...♔h6?

After 34...♔g8, White could have
serious problems. For example:
35.♖xf8+ ♖xf8 36.♖xf8+ ♔xf8 37.h3
♕b1+ 38.♔h2 ♕b7, and Black is
better.

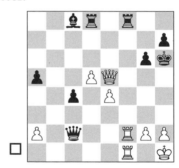

**White has a very powerful move
here. Can you spot it?**

35.♕e7?

Playing for a draw, but 35.♖f4! ♗g4
(35...♖xf4 36.♕xf4+ ♔h5 (36...♔g7
37.♕f6+ ♔h6 38.♕h4+ ♔g7
39.♕xd8+−) 37.g3! ♗g4 38.h3 ♕e2
39.♖f2! ♕d1+ 40.♔h2 ♖d7 41.♕f6
♔h6 42.hxg4 ♕xg4 43.♖f4+−)
36.h4! c3 37.♕g5+ ♔g7 38.♕e7+ ♔h6
39.♖xf8 was winning.

35...♖xf2 36.♕h4+ ♔g7 37.♕e7+ ♔h6 38.♕h4+ ♔g7 39.♕e7+ ♔h6 40.♕h4+ ½-½

Haik Martirosyan   2391
Bulat Nizamov   2092

European Youth Chess Championship
Batumi 2014 (U14 Open)

How does Black deal best with the threats against the f7-pawn?

19...♖ed8!

The alternatives are worse:

A) 19...♖ad8? 20.♗xf7+ ♕xf7 21.♖xd8 ♖xd8 22.♕xd8+ ♔g7 23.♗c5 ♗f6 24.♗d4+−;

B) 19...♔h8?! 20.♗xf7 ♖ec8 21.♗e7 ♕b2 22.♕d4+ ♕xd4 23.exd4 ♖c1+ 24.♔h2 ♖c6 25.♗g5±

20.♗xf7+

How is Black supposed to keep his position together?

20...♔g7!

A) Not 20...♕xf7? 21.♖xd8+ ♖xd8 22.♕xd8+ ♔g7 23.♗c5, with a clear advantage to White;

B) The game continued with 20...♔h8? 21.♗e7 ♕xf7 22.♕xa1+ ♔g8 23.♖xd8+ ♖xd8 24.♗xd8+−.

21.♗e7

21.♗c4+ ♔h6 22.♗e2 ♗e5=

21...♕xe7 22.♕xa1+ ♕f6 23.♕xf6+ ♔xf6 24.♖xb7 ♖d2 25.♗c4 ♖xa2 26.♖f7+ ♔e5 27.♖xh7

With chances for both sides.

Awonder Liang   2365
Luka Budisavljevic   2093

World Youth Chess Championship
Halkidiki 2015 (U12 Open)

1.e4 c5 2.♘f3 e6 3.d4 cxd4 4.♘xd4 a6 5.♗d3 ♗c5 6.♘b3 ♗a7 7.0-0 ♘e7 8.♕e2 0-0 9.♗e3 ♘bc6 10.♘c3 b5 11.a3 ♕c7 12.♔h1 ♗xe3 13.♕xe3 ♗b7 14.f4 e5 15.♘d5 ♕d6 16.♘xe7+?!

Better was 16.♘c5.

16...♕xe7 17.f5

Things are starting to look scary for Black. Play the right move, a prophylactic one.

17...d6?

Black had to prevent the next move with 17...f6, with only a small advantage to White. Perhaps Black feared 18.♘c5, but after 18...d6 19.♘xb7 ♛xb7, nothing special happens.

18.f6! gxf6 19.♛h6 ♗c8 20.♖xf6 ♗e6 21.♘d2

How should Black defend?

21...♘b8?
Black had to drive away the most dangerous white piece, namely the queen, with 21...♖fe8 (21...♚h8? 22.♘f3 ♖g8 23.♘g5 ♖g7 24.♘xe6 fxe6 25.♖xe6) 22.♘f3 (or 22.♖af1 ♛f8 23.♛e3 ♘b8 24.c4 ♘d7) 22...♛f8 23.♘g5 ♛xh6 24.♖xh6 b4. White is better, but Black can fight. Now, it's all over.

How can White continue the attack?

22.♘f3!+– ♘d7 23.♘g5 ♘xf6 24.♖f1 ♖fe8 25.♖xf6 ♛a7 26.♖xh7 ♗f5 27.♖xf5 f6 28.♘xf6+ ♚f7 29.♘d5+

♚g8 30.♖g5+ ♚f7 31.♖g7+ ♚f8 32.♛h8# 1-0

Alserkal Rouda Essa   1250
Iris Mou

World Cadets Chess Championship (U8 Girls),
Poços de Caldas 2017

Find Black's best move.

41...♛a1+?
It was necessary to defend with 41...♛b6! 42.♖xc7 ♛xa7 43.♖xa7 ♗b5 44.♖c7 ♖d8 45.♖c1 ♖d2 46.♗b1 ♚g7 47.♚g1 a3−+.
42.♘f1 ♛xf1+ 43.♚h2

How must Black defend?

43...♖e8?
Black had to play 43...♛b5! 44.♖xc7 (44.♛xc7 ♛b7 45.♖xe7 ♛xc7 46.♖xc7 ♖b7 47.♖c8+ ♚e7 48.♖g8 ♖b6=) 44...♛b7, fighting on the seventh rank. For example: 45.♖c8+

♔g7 46.♕a8 ♕xe5 47.♖g8+ ♔h7
48.♕xa6 ♕g5 49.♕xb7 ♕g3+ 50.♔h1
♕e1+=

44.♕xc7?
After 44.♕d4 ♔g7 45.♕xf4, White
has a strong attack, for example:
45...♕b5 (45...♕e2 46.♗b1 ♔g8
47.♗xg6) 46.♕f6+ ♔h6 47.♖xe7
♖xe7 48.♕xe7+–

How must Black continue?

44...♕f2?
Perhaps Black was happy with a
draw or had little time. Better was
44...♖c8! 45.♕b6 ♕e1 46.♕xg6
♕g3+ 47.♕xg3 fxg3+ 48.♔xg3 a3,
with good winning chances.

45.♖xe7!

45...♕g3+
45...♖xe7? 46.♕d8+ ♔g7 47.♕xe7+
♔h6 48.♕f8+ ♔g5 49.♕f6+ ♔h6
50.♕xf4+ ♔h7 51.♕f7+ ♔h6
52.♕f8+ ♔g5 53.♗b1 a3 54.♕f6+
♔h6 55.♕xg6#

46.♔g1 ♕e1+ 47.♔h2 ♕g3+
48.♔g1 ♕e1+ ½-½

Later, White won the gold medal,
while Black finished in seventh
place.

Felix Blohberger   2256
Semen Lomasov   2393
World Youth Chess Championship
Khanty-Mansiysk 2016 (U14 Open)

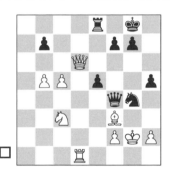

**White's king is in danger. Can you
find a way out?**

29.♖h1?
White played this move after
a few seconds. There were two
good moves that required precise
calculation:
   A) 29.♘e4! ♕xh2+ 30.♔f1 f5?!
(30...♕f4 31.♔e2 ♘h2 32.♗h1)
31.♕g6! ♖a8 32.♖d7+–;
   B) 29.♕d2 ♕xh2+ 30.♔f1 ♕h3+
31.♗g2 ♘h2+ 32.♔g1 ♘f3+ 33.♗xf3
♕xf3 34.♕d3 ♕g4+ 35.♕g3, and
White is better.
Perhaps White decided to play so
passively for time reasons (he had
a dozen minutes for twelve moves),
but this time an active move was
the better defence.

29...h4!

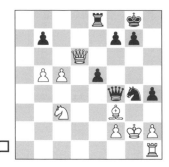

How can White defend best?

30.♕d3?!

A) Not 30.h3? ♘e3+! 31.fxe3
♕g3++−;

B) It was correct to play 30.♕d1!
h3+ 31.♔f1 (31.♔g1 ♘e3 32.fxe3
♕xe3+ 33.♔f1 ♕xc3 34.♗xb7 e4)
31...♕c4+ 32.♘e2 ♘f6 33.♖g1, with a
complicated position.

30...h3+ 31.♔f1

31.♔g1?? e4! 32.♕e2 ♘f6 33.♗g2
♕g5−+

31...e4 32.♘xe4 ♘e5 33.♕e3 ♕xf3

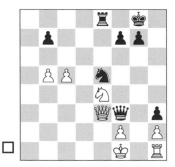

What is your move with white?

34.♖g1?

He had to play 34.♕xf3 ♘xf3 35.♔e2
♘g5 36.f3 f5 37.♖g1 ♘f7 38.♔e3 fxe4
39.fxe4 ♘e5 40.♖g3, with a worse
endgame, but drawing chances.

34...♕d1+ 35.♔e1 ♕d3+ 36.♕e2
♕b1+ 37.♕e1 ♕xb5+ 38.♕e2
♕b1+ 39.♕e1 ♕xe1+ 0-1

Semen Lomasov won the gold.

Leon Luke Mendonca 2133
Mikhail Spizharny 1760

World Cadets Chess Championship
Batumi 2016 (U10 Open)

Black is two pawns down and must make an important decision. To take or not to take the ♗g6?

20...♗h2+!

The game continued with 20...fxg6?
21.♕xg6 ♖e7 22.♖xe7 ♕xe7, and
here White had to play 23.g3!. For
example: 23...♗a6 24.c4 ♗b4 25.♔g2
♕h7 26.♖h1, with a great advantage
for White.

21.♔h1 ♗f4 22.♘f3 fxg6

What is your move with white?

23.g3!

Not 23.♕xg6 in view of 23...♕h7+
24.♕xh7+ ♔xh7, and the two

bishops are stronger than the knight and three pawns.

23...♗d6 24.♔g2 ♕g7 25.♘h4

With a complicated position. For example:

25...♔g8 26.♘xg6 ♖e4 27.♖xe4 dxe4 28.♕xe4 ♕f7 29.f3 ♖e8 30.♕d3 c5
With a nearly balanced position.

The next game was played in the final round of the WSCC and decided the bronze medal.

Teodor-Cosmin Nedelcu   1682
Taha Ozkan   1572
World School Chess Championship
Iasi 2017 (U11 Open)

Only one move can save Black. Do you see it?

The game continued with
50...♕c3+?
Black had to threaten a perpetual check, while keeping the white advanced pawn under attack: 50...♕b3!, and now:

analysis diagram

A) 51.e7 ♕e3+ 52.♔d1 ♕b3+ 53.♔c1 ♕c3+ 54.♔d1 ♕b3+ 55.♔e1 ♕e3+ 56.♔f1 ♕f3+ 57.♔g1 ♕e3+=;

B) 51.♕c6+ ♔d4 (or 51...♔e5=, but not 51...♔e3? 52.♕c1+) 52.♕d7+ ♔e4 53.♕b7+ ♔e3 54.♕b6+ ♔e4=, since White has no time to push the pawn.

51.♕d2 ♕c8
51...♕a1+ 52.♔e2 ♕g1 53.e7 ♕xh2+ 54.♔d1+−

52.e7 b3

53.e8♕+ ♕xe8 54.♕e2+ 1-0

CHAPTER 9

Test

Here are fifty positions for you to solve. You must indicate the correct first move and state the idea behind it. Sometimes, it will be the winning move, other times the drawing move or the move that causes the greatest problems to the opponent.

I suggest that you acquaint yourself with each position, and find the candidate moves before calculating. It's preferable to use a chessboard and give yourself 10 minutes for each position. A good idea is to solve a few puzzles (five, for example) every day and look at the solutions. By doing this, you can see how well you are going, and you'll learn something that may be possible to apply in the following days.

After a few weeks, try to solve all the puzzles you didn't solve correctly (both the exercises given in the illustrative games and the ones given here), this time giving yourself only five minutes for each one. After a few months, read this book again and try to solve all the puzzles. To learn a skill, it has to be repeated several times.

Exercise 41

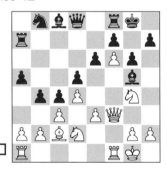

(Solution on page 115)

Exercise 42

(Solution on page 115)

Exercise 43

(Solution on page 115)

Exercise 44

(Solution on page 116)

Exercise 45

(Solution on page 116)

Exercise 46

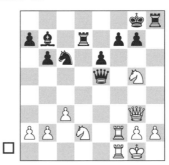

(Solution on page 116)

Exercise 47

(Solution on page 117)

Exercise 48

(Solution on page 117)

Exercise 49

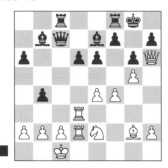

(Solution on page 117)

Exercise 50

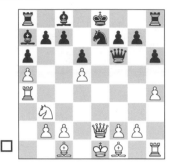

(Solution on page 118)

Exercise 51

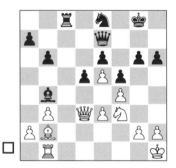

(Solution on page 118)

Exercise 52

(Solution on page 119)

Exercise 53

(Solution on page 119)

Exercise 54

(Solution on page 119)

Exercise 55

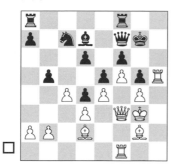

(Solution on page 120)

Exercise 56

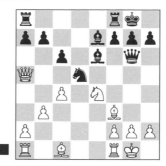

(Solution on page 120)

Exercise 57

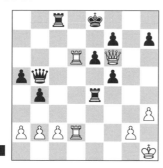

(Solution on page 120)

Exercise 58

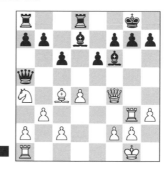

(Solution on page 121)

Exercise 59

(Solution on page 121)

Exercise 60

(Solution on page 121)

Exercise 61

(Solution on page 122)

Exercise 62

(Solution on page 122)

Exercise 63

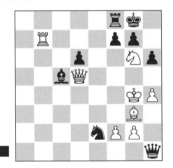

(Solution on page 123)

Exercise 64

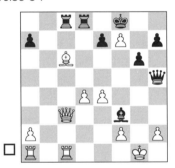

(Solution on page 123)

Exercise 65

(Solution on page 124)

Exercise 66

(Solution on page 124)

Exercise 67

(Solution on page 125)

Exercise 68

(Solution on page 125)

Exercise 69

(Solution on page 125)

Exercise 70

(Solution on page 126)

Exercise 71

(Solution on page 126)

Exercise 72

(Solution on page 127)

Exercise 73

(Solution on page 127)

Exercise 74

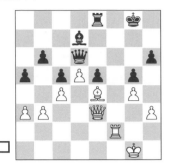

(Solution on page 128)

Exercise 75

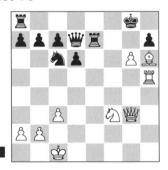

(Solution on page 128)

Exercise 76

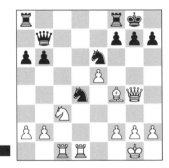

(Solution on page 129)

Exercise 77

(Solution on page 129)

Exercise 78

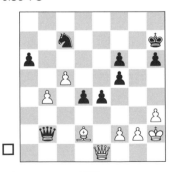

(Solution on page 129)

Exercise 79

(Solution on page 130)

Exercise 80

(Solution on page 130)

Exercise 81

(Solution on page 131)

Exercise 82

(Solution on page 131)

Exercise 83

(Solution on page 131)

Exercise 84

(Solution on page 132)

Exercise 85

(Solution on page 132)

Exercise 86

(Solution on page 133)

Exercise 87

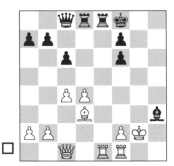

(Solution on page 133)

Exercise 88

(Solution on page 133)

Exercise 89

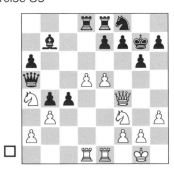

(Solution on page 134)

Exercise 90

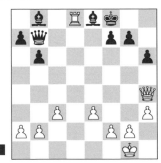

(Solution on page 135)

CHAPTER 10

Solutions

Solution 41

Grigori Ponomarev   1978
Umid Aslanov   1651

European Youth Chess Championship
Prague 2016 (U10 Open)

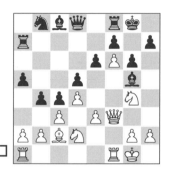

19.h4! ♗xh4 20.♕f4
With a double threat to the king
(♕h6) and the knight.
20...g5 21.♕xb8+−

Solution 42

Toivo Keinanen   2337
Or Globus   2165

European Youth Chess Championship
Prague 2016 (U14 Open)

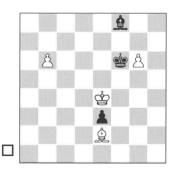

125.g7!

A) With the same idea, it was
possible to play 125.♔d5 ♗h6 126.
g7! ♔xg7 127.♔e4 ♗g5 128.b7+−;
B) The game continued with
125.♗d3? e2 126.♗xe2 ♔xg6 127.♔d5
♗h6 128.♔e5 ♗g7+ 129.♔d5 ♗h6=.
125...♔xg7
125...♗xg7 126.b7+−
126.♔d5 ♔f7 127.b7+−
The 'execution' can appear at any
moment. Here, it appeared at move
125, and unfortunately it does not
inform us of its arrival.

Solution 43

Nameer Issani   1900
Jason Wang   1999

World Cadets Chess Championship
Batumi 2016 (U10 Open)

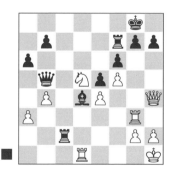

29...♖f2!
Not 29...♕e2? 30.♕g4 ♕xg4 31.♖xg4
♖a2 32.♖g3∓, and neither, as in the
game, 29...♔h8? 30.♕g4=.
30.♖g1
30.♖f3 ♖xf3 31.gxf3 ♕e2−+
30...♖f1 31.♘e3 ♖xg1+ 32.♔xg1
♕e2−+

Solution 44
Davaakhuu Munkhzul   1808
Emilia Zavivaeva   1492
World Cadets Chess Championship
Batumi 2016 (U10 Girls)

18.♘xf7!
18.♕f3 ♘d8
18...♚xf7?
18...♖f8 19.♗xf8 ♖xf8 20.♘c3 ♚xf7
21.♘xd5+−
19.♕f3+ ♚e6?
19...♚g8 20.♗xd5+ ♕xd5 21.♘f6+
♗xf6 22.♕xd5++−
20.♕g4+ ♚f7 21.♕xd7 ♗c8
22.♗xd5# 1-0

Solution 45
Andrey Tsvetkov   2096
Georg Aleksander Pedoson   1944
European Youth Chess Championship
Prague 2016 (U12 Open)

35...♖c1!

The game continued with 35...♖c8?
36.♗c5, and White won.
36.♖f2
Or 36.♗b2 (36.♗c5?? g5!−+) 36...♖b1
37.♕d4 ♕f7 38.♗f3 ♕g6 39.♖d1
♗e4 40.♕xe4 ♕xe4 41.♗xe4 ♖xd1
42.♚h3 ♖d2 43.♗c1 ♖d4 44.♗g6
♖xd5, with advantage to Black.
36...g5!
Attacking on the first rank and on
the h-file.
37.♖f1 ♖xf1 38.♗xf1 gxf4 39.g4!
♗e4 40.♗xf6 ♕xg4
With advantage to Black, for
example:
41.♕d8+ ♚f7 42.♗h4 ♕g6
43.♕d7+ ♚f8 44.♕d8+ ♚g7
45.♕d7+ ♚h6 46.♕h3 ♗f5

Solution 46
Shageldi Kurbandurdyew   1240
Raul Mukhtarov   1442
World Cadets Chess Championship
Batumi 2016 (U8 Open)

28.♖xf7!
The game continued with 28.♘xf7?
♕xg3 29.hxg3, and here Black,
instead of 29...♖d5? 30.♘xh8+−,
could play 29...♖h5 30.g4 ♖hd5,
with a good position.
28...♖xf7 29.♖xf7 ♕xg3 30.hxg3
♗a6 31.♖c7
Black's position is cramped.

**31...♘d8 32.♖d7 ♘c6 33.b4 ♔f8
34.♘de4 ♗c8 35.♖f7+ ♔e8 36.♘d6+
♔d8 37.♖xg7+–**

Shageldi Kurbandurdyew finished
clear first with 9.5 out of 11.

Solution 47
Nikhil Kumar 2076
Rameshbabu Praggnanandhaa 2442
World Cadets Chess Championship
Batumi 2016 (U12 Open)

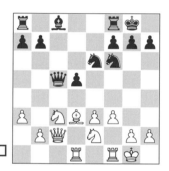

16.♘xd5! ♘xd5
Or 16...♕xc2 17.♘xf6+ gxf6
18.♗xc2+–.
17.♗xh7+ ♔h8

**18.♕xc5 ♘xc5 19.♖xd5 ♔xh7
20.♖xc5**
And White won.

Kumar won the title, and
Praggnanandhaa took the bronze.

Solution 48
Liam Vrolijk 2221
Lukas Bango 2058
European Youth Chess Championship
Prague 2016 (U14 Open)

34.d5! cxd5?
34...♕f5 35.♖f4 ♕g6 36.♕a6 ♖bb8
37.dxc6+–
**35.♗g4 ♖xc4 36.♗xe6 ♖b8 37.♕xa7
1-0**

Solution 49
Mihail Nikitenko 2295
Hrvoje Pozgaj 1990
European Youth Chess Championship
Batumi 2014 (U14 Open)

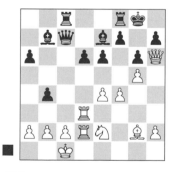

20...f6?
Better was 20...f5! 21.♘d4 ♖f7!. The
rook defends the seventh rank and
Black can counterattack (21...♕d7 is
not bad: 22.exf5 exf5 23.♗xb7 ♕xb7
24.♖e2 ♖f7 25.♕h3, with only a

slight advantage to White): 22.exf5 (22.♘xe6 ♕b6 gives complicated play. For example: 23.♖d4 fxe4 24.f5 e3 25.fxg6 exd2+ 26.♔xd2 ♗xg2 27.gxf7+ ♔xf7 28.♕h5+ ♔xe6 29.♕g4+ ♔f7 30.♖f4+ ♔g7 31.♕xc8 ♕c5 32.♕e6 ♗xg5 33.♕f7+ ♔h6 34.♕e6+ ♔h5 35.♕f7+ ♔h6=) 22...exf5 23.♘e6 ♕d7 24.♗xb7 ♕xb7 25.♖e2 ♕h1+ 26.♖d1 ♕f3 27.♖de1 d5, with chances for both sides. Now, instead of 21.♘d4?! (the game continued with 21...♕d7? 22.f5! exf5 23.exf5 ♖f7 24.fxg6 hxg6 25.♗h3 ♕a4 26.♗e6 ♗e4 27.♖h3 1-0, but Black should have played 21...♖f7), White could play

21.f5! ♖fe8

21...fxg5 22.fxg6 ♗f6 23.♘d4 ♕g7 24.♕xg7+ ♗xg7 25.♘xe6

22.fxg6 ♗f8 23.♕xh7+ ♕xh7 24.gxh7+ ♔xh7 25.♖h3+ ♔g6 26.♘f4+ ♔xg5 27.♖f2

With a clear advantage.

Solution 50
Gonzalo Quirhuayo Chumbe 2272
Camilo Corredor Castellanos 1918
World Youth Chess Championship
Durban 2014 (U12 Open)

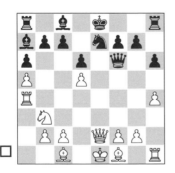

14.♖f4!

The game continued with 14.g4?! (14.♗g5?? hxg5 15.hxg5 ♕xf2+

16.♕xf2 ♗xf2+ 17.♔xf2 ♖xh1–+) 14...0-0, with unclear play.

14...♕g6

15.♖e4

15.h5!? ♕g5 16.♖xf7 ♕e5 17.♕xe5 dxe5 18.♖xg7+–

15...♕f6 16.♗d2 0-0 17.♖xe7 ♗g4 18.f3 ♗e6 19.♖xc7 ♗xd5 20.♗c3+–

Solution 51
Ekaterine Pipia 1583
Jovana Srdanovic 1737
European Youth Chess Championship
Porec 2015 (U12 Girls)

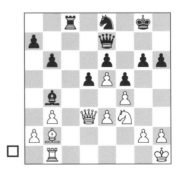

29.a3! ♗xa3

It was better to play 29...♗c5, although White has a clear advantage after 30.b4 ♗xb4 31.axb4 ♕xb4 32.♗d4 ♕f8 33.♖a1.

30.♕a6 ♗xb2 31.♕xc8 ♗a3 32.♘d4+–

Solution 52

Leonid Lystsov	1885
Adam Mekhane	1967

World Cadets Chess Championship
Poços de Caldas 2017 (U10 Open)

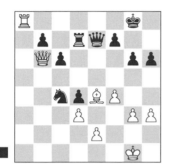

40...♔g7?
40...♔h7! 41.♕a7! (otherwise, White is clearly worse) 41...f5 42.♕b8 ♕g7 43.♗xc6 bxc6 44.dxc4, with an even game. For example: 44...d3 45.exd3 ♖xd3 46.♖a7 ♖d7 47.♖xd7 ♕xd7=
41.♕a7 f5 42.♕b8 ♔f6 43.♕g8 ♘d6 44.♖f8+ ♘f7 45.♗f3

White has a strong attack. The game continued with
45...h5
45...♖c7 46.♖e8 ♕b4 47.♔f2 ♖e7 48.♖f8 ♖c7 49.g4 ♕e7 50.gxf5 gxf5 51.♗h5+−
46.♔g2 ♖d6 47.g4 hxg4 48.hxg4 ♕e6 49.g5+ ♔e7 50.♖e8+ ♔d7 51.♖xe6 ♖xe6 52.♕xf7++−

Solution 53

Martyna Wikar	1803
Noam Portnoy	1710

European Youth Chess Championship
Prague 2016 (U12 Girls)

27...♔h8??
27...♗xh6 28.♕xh6 ♕e5=
28.♘xg6+! hxg6 29.♘f5+ 1-0
29...♔g8 30.♘e7#

Solution 54

Nutakki Priyanka	2042
Mitzy Mishe Caballero Quijano	1848

World Youth Championship
Halkidiki 2015 (U14 Girls)

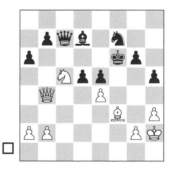

38.♕b6+!
And Black resigned.

Solution 55

Aravind Ram 2085
Matey Petkov 1912

World Youth Chess Championship

Durban 2014 (U12 Open)

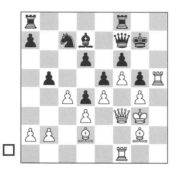

25.♗xg5! ♖h8

The game continued with 25...fxg5
26.♖fh1 ♕e8 27.f6+ ♔g8 28.♖h8+
♔f7 29.♖1h7+ ♔g6 30.♖g7#.

26.♗xf6+!

26...♔xf6

26...♕xf6 27.g5 ♕d8 (27...♕f7 28.f6+
♔g8 29.♖xh8+ ♔xh8 30.♖h1+
♔g8 31.♖h6 ♘e8 32.♕f1+–) 28.f6+
♔f7 29.♖xh8 ♕xh8 30.♖h1 ♕g8
31.♕h5+ ♕g6 32.♕h7+ ♕xh7
33.♖xh7+ ♔g8 34.♖g7+ ♔h8
35.♖xd7+–

**27.g5+ ♔g7 28.f6+ ♔g8 29.♖xh8+
♔xh8 30.♖h1+ ♔g8 31.♖h6 ♘e8
32.♕f1+–**

Solution 56

Anastasia Kozina 1988
Qiyu Zhou 2119

World Youth Chess Championship

Durban 2014 (U14 Girls)

17...♗b4!

The game continued with 17...♘f6=.
18.♕a4 a5 19.cxd5

19.♗d2 ♘b6–+

**19...♗xd5 20.♗a3 b5 21.♗xb4 bxa4
22.♗xf8 ♔xf8 23.♘d2 axb3 24.axb3
♕d3 25.♗xd5 cxd5–+**

Solution 57

Ashritha Eswaran 1977
Alexandra Obolentseva 2151

World Youth Chess Championship

Durban 2014 (U14 Girls)

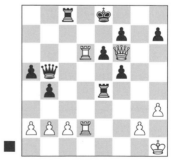

Certainly, you saw that after
28...♖e1+ 29.♔h2 ♕e5+ 30.♕xe5
♖xe5 31.♖d7 ♖ec5 32.♖a7 ♖8c7,
Black has a better endgame, but the

game is not clearly won. The game went in this way, and Black won after nearly thirty moves. There was a much better solution:
28...♕f1+! 29.♔h2 ♕f4+ 30.g3

30...♕xd6! 31.♖xd6 ♖xc2+ 32.♔g1 ♖e1#

Solution 58
Maxim Bellver Gorshenin 1437
Killian Diaz Reyes 1296
Spanish Youth Championship
Salobreña 2016 (U10)

54...♕f5!
Now, Black has no more problems in defence and his threats are difficult to face. The game continued with 54...♔h8? 55.♘c5 ♗c8 56.c3 ♖f8 57.♘e4, and White was better.
55.♕d2
55.♕xf5 exf5 56.♗f1 ♗xd4 57.♖d1 ♗e6
55...b5 56.♗d3 ♕d5 57.♘c3 ♕xd4 58.♖d1 g6∓

Solution 59
Ekin Baris Ozenir 2030
Vladislav Larkin 1932
European Youth Chess Championship
Prague 2016 (U12 Open)

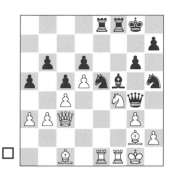

25.♖xe5!
The game continued with 25.♖e3?±.
25...dxe5 26.♗f3 ♕g5
26...♕xf3 27.♕xf3 ♗d7 28.♗b2 exf4 29.♕c3 ♖f6 30.♖e1+−
27.♘e6
27.♘xh5 ♕e7 is less promising.
27...♕f6 28.♗g5 ♕f7 29.♘xf8 ♖xf8 30.♗xh5 gxh5 31.♕xe5+−

Solution 60
Artem Trubchaninov 2071
David Gavrilescu 2346
European Youth Chess Championship
Mamaia 2017 (U14 Open)

28...♗xg4!

In this position, where Black doesn't have much else, it shouldn't be difficult to find the right move.

29.♘h6+?

After 29.♔e1 ♗xf5 30.exf5 ♔g7 31.♕b2 ♕h8 32.♕f2 ♔f6, Black is winning, but at least White can try to resist a little.

29...♔g7 30.♘xg4 ♕h8

31.♘e3?

31.♔e1 ♕h4+ 32.♔d2 ♕xg4 33.♔c2 ♕g2+ 34.♔b3 ♕xh2−+

31...♕xh2+ 32.♔f3 ♕e2+ 33.♔g3 ♕xe3+ 0-1

The white king is mated in two moves.

Solution 61
Barbara Goraj 1619
Eva Stepanyan 1780
European Youth Chess Championship
Prague 2016 (U12 Girls)

15...♗xh3!

Black played 15...♘h5?!, with only a small plus.

16.gxh3

Or 16.♖fe1 ♕d7 17.♗f1 ♗g4−+.

16...♕d7 17.♔g2 d4!

18.♖fe1

  A) 18.♘xd4 ♘h4+ 19.♔g1 ♕xh3 20.♗f3 ♕h2#;

  B) 18.♗xd4 ♖xe2−+ (18...♘f4+−+)

18...dxe3 19.fxe3 ♕f5

With a strong attack. For example:

20.♗f1 ♘h5 21.♘c3 ♘h4+ 22.♘xh4 ♕g5+ 23.♔f3 ♕xh4−+

Solution 62
Javokhir Sindarov 2299
Quoc Hy Nguyen 1583
World Youth Chess Championship
Halkidiki 2015 (U10 Open)

19...♖ec8?

19...♕d5! 20.♔g2 g5 21.h3 h5 22.g4 hxg4 23.hxg4 f5 24.gxf5 g4−+

20.♖c1 ♕d5 21.♔g2 ♖c6

It's too late for 21...g5?! 22.♖he1 g4 23.♖xe7±.

22.♖he1 ♖f6 23.♖e4 ♖xf3 24.♖xe7

24...♖xg3+

Or 24...♖e3+ 25.♖e4 ♖xe4 26.dxe4 ♕xe4+ 27.♔g1=.

25.♔xg3?!

Better was 25.♔f1!, with an even game. For example: 25...♕g2+ 26.♔e1 ♖e3+ 27.fxe3 ♕g1+ 28.♔e2 ♕xh2+ 29.♔f1 ♕h1+ 30.♔e2 ♕g2+ 31.♔e1=

25...♕g5+ 26.♔f3 ♕f6+ 27.♔g2 ♕xe7

Black is better.

Solution 63
Semen Lomasov 2383
Shant Sargsyan 2441
European Youth Chess Championship
Prague 2016 (U14 Open)

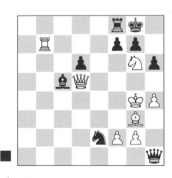

40...♘c3!

The game went 40...h5+? 41.♔xh5 ♘xg3+ (41...♘c3 42.♕xf7+! ♖xf7 43.♖b8+ ♔f8 44.♖xf8+ ♔h7 45.♖h8#) 42.fxg3 ♕f1 43.♘xf8 ♔xf8 44.♖b8+ ♔e7 45.♕e4+ ♔f6 46.g4 g5 47.♖g8 1-0. This was the 40th move, and Black had nearly one minute left.

41.♘e7+

41.♕b3 ♕xg2 42.♖xf7 (42.♘xf8? h5+ 43.♔g5 ♗e3+ 44.fxe3 ♕xg3+ 45.♔xh5 ♕f3+ 46.♔g5 ♘e4#) 42...♖xf7 43.♘e7+ ♔f8 44.♘g6+ ♔g8=

41...♔h8 42.♕f3 ♕d1=

Solution 64
Nikoloz Petriashvili 2198
Jan Pultorak 2296
European Youth Chess Championship
Prague 2016 (U14 Open)

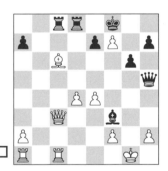

27.♕e3!

Only move. White defends both the ♙f2 and the ♙e4. The game went 27.♔f1? ♖xc6! (27...♗xe4 28.d5 ♖xc6! 29.dxc6 ♗d3–+) 28.♕xc6 ♕xh2 29.♔e1 ♕g1+ 30.♔d2 ♕xf2+ 31.♔c3 ♕xd4+ 0-1.

27...♕g4+

Other possibilities:

A) 27...♕h3?! 28.♕g5 ♖xd4 29.♗d5±;

B) 27...♖xc6 28.♖xc6 ♕g4+ 29.♔f1
♕g2+ 30.♔e1 ♕h1+ 31.♔d2 ♕xa1
32.♕h6+ ♔xf7 33.♕xh7+ ♔e8
34.♕g8+ ♔d7 35.♕e6+ ♔e8=;

C) 27...e5 28.♗d5 exd4 29.♕f4
♕h3 30.♕g5 d3 31.♖c3 d2 32.♖xf3
♕xf3 33.♕h6+ ♔e7 34.♕xd2 ♕g4+
35.♔f1 ♕h3+ 36.♔g1=;

D) 27...g5 28.♗d7 ♖xc1+ 29.♕xc1
♗xe4 30.♕c7 ♖a8 31.♕g3=

**28.♔f1 ♔xf7 29.♔e1 ♖b8 30.♗d5+
♔g7 31.♔d2 ♖b2+ 32.♖c2 ♖xc2+
33.♔xc2 e6 34.♗b3 ♗xe4+ 35.♔b2
♖f8 36.♖e1 ♗d5**

With only a minimal advantage to
Black.

Solution 65
Mihajlo Radovanovic   2421
Viachaslau Zarubitski   2310

European Youth Chess Championship
Porec 2015 (U14 Open)

40.♖ce1?
The fatal 40th move. White could
easily draw with 40.♖cc2! (probably,
White was focused on defending
and didn't consider Black's weak
king position) 40...♖xc2 (40...♖8b7
41.♕a8+ ♖b8 42.♕a7=) 41.♕xb8+
♔h7 42.♖xc2 ♕xc2+ 43.♔g3. For
example: 43...♕d3 44.♔h2 ♕xa3
45.♕xd6 ♕xe3 46.♕e5 g6 47.♕e7+
♔h6 48.♕g5+ ♔g7 49.♕e7+ ♔h6=

40...♖8b3 41.♕a8+?!
41.♕d7 ♕xe3+ 42.♔f1 ♕xf4+
43.♔g1 ♕e5–+
41...♔h7 42.♔f1?!
42.♖xb2 ♖xb2+ 43.♔g3 ♕d2 44.♖g1
♕xe3+ 45.♔h2 ♕xf4++–
42...♖xe2 43.♖xe2 ♖b2 0-1

Solution 66
Andrey Esipenko   2384
Patryk Chylewski   2161

World Youth Chess Championship
Halkidiki 2015 (U14 Open)

30...♗xe4+?
After this move, the white bishop
can come into the attack. The
right move was 30...♗xb1!, with
an even game: 31.♕xf7+ ♔h8
32.♕f6+ (32.♗c4 ♗xe4+ 33.♔f2
♖b7 34.♕f6+ ♔h7 35.♕g6+ ♔h8
36.♕h6+ ♖h7 37.♕f6+ ♖g7=; 32.♗f3
♗xa2 33.♕h5+ ♔g8 34.♕g6+
♔f8 35.♕xd6+ ♔g8 36.♕g6+ ♔f8
37.♕f6+ ♔g8=) 32...♔g8 33.♕g6+
♔h8 34.♕h6+ ♔g8 35.♕xg5+ ♔h8
36.♕h6+ ♔g8
**31.♗f3! ♗xb1 32.♕xf7+ ♔h8
33.♕f6+ ♔h7 34.♕g6+ ♔h8
35.♕h6+ 1-0**
(35...♔g8 36.♗d5#)

Andrey Esipenko finished 1st-2nd
(second on tiebreak).

Solution 67

Kazybek Nogerbek   2162
Ganzorig Amartuvshin   1909

World Cadets Chess Championship
Batumi 2016 (U12 Open)

The game continued with 19...♘a8 20.a3 b6 21.b4 ♕c8, with a roughly even position. On the third rank, seven squares are occupied by White's pawns and pieces. Perhaps something is wrong? It is possible to attack the g3-pawn with 19...♘h5, but White is OK after 20.♗f2!. But look at those four white pieces on the second and third ranks. Aren't they on weak squares, which can be attacked by the black pieces? Black only needs to open the play with **19...d5!! 20.exd5**

  A) 20.♘xd5 ♘fxd5 21.exd5 (21. cxd5 ♕xd3 22.♗xd3 ♗xa1 23.♖xa1 ♘xd5 24.♗h6 ♘b4 25.♗c4 ♘d3–+) 21...♖xe3 22.♕xe3 ♗d4 23.♕xd4 cxd4 24.dxc6 bxc6–+;

  B) 20.cxd5 ♕xd3 21.♗xd3 ♘fxd5 22.♘xd5 ♗xa1 23.♖xa1 ♘xd5–+

20...♘fxd5 21.♘xd5

21.cxd5 ♕xd3 22.♗xd3 ♗xc3 23.dxc6 ♗xa1 24.♗e4 ♗c3 25.♖e2 bxc6–+

21...♗xd5 22.cxd5 ♕xd3 23.♗xd3 ♗xa1 24.♘e4 ♘xd5 25.♖xa1 ♘xe3 26.♘f6+ ♔f8 27.♘xe8 ♖xd3 28.♘f6 ♖d2–+

Solution 68

Hagawane Aakanksha   1909
Shengxin Zhao   1766

World Youth Chess Championship
Durban 2014 (U14 Girls)

18.♗xc2!

The game went 18.♕xc2? (18.♔f1?? ♕a4 19.♗xc2 ♖xc2–+) 18...♕a3 19.♗c4 ♖xc4! 20.♕xc4 ♖c8 21.♘c7 ♗e6 22.♕c6 ♕xb4+ 23.♔f1 ♕c4+ 24.♕xc4 ♗xc4+∓.

18...♕xa6 19.b5 ♕a5+ 20.♕b4 ♗d8 21.♗d3 ♕xb4+ 22.♘xb4 ♗a5 23.a3

White has a small plus.

Solution 69

Stefan Raykov   2022
Quentin Burri   2279

European Youth Chess Championship
Porec 2015 (U14 Open)

38...♖xg5?

38...♗xc1! 39.♖c8! ♕d5 (39...♕b7
40.♖f2 ♔e7 41.♖g8 ♔f7 42.♖d8 ♖f4
43.♕e2 ♔e7 44.♖d4 ♘h4+ 45.♔h3
♘f5 46.♖xf4 ♗xf4 47.♕xc4 ♘xd4
48.♕xd4 ♔f7=) 40.♖c5 ♖f4 41.♕h5
♕d1 42.♖c7+ ♔g8 43.♖c8+ ♔f7=
39.♕xg5 ♗xg5 40.♖c8! ♕xc8
40...♕b7 41.♗xg5+–
**41.♘d6+ ♔g8 42.♘xc8 ♗xc1
43.♖e4 ♗d2 44.♘xa7 ♗xc3 45.♖xc4
♗d2 46.a4+–**
And White won.

Solution 70
Margarita Zvereva   1930
Eline Roebers
European Youth Chess Championship
Prague 2016 (U10 Girls)

14...♘xd3!
 A) Not 14...g5? 15.♖xf6 ♖xe5
16.♖f3+–;
 B) The game went 14...♖xe5?
15.♘xc6! ♗g4 16.♘xd8 ♗xd1
17.♖axd1 ♖e8 18.♘xf7! ♔xf7 19.♘d5
♖ac8 20.♘xf6 gxf6 21.♖xf6+ ♔g8
22.♖g6+ 1-0.
15.♕xd3
Not 15.exf6?! ♕xd4 16.♗g3 ♖e3
17.♗f4 ♖xh3+ 18.gxh3 ♘f2+ 19.♖xf2
♕xf2 20.fxg7 ♗e7, and Black is
better.
15...♖xe5 16.♗xf6 gxf6
With chances for both sides.

Margarita Zvereva finished 1st-2nd
(silver medal on tiebreak).

Solution 71
Andrey Tsvetkov   2219
Matei-Stefan Vilcu   1977
European Youth Chess Championship
Mamaia 2017 (U12 Open)

27.♘xd6!
White played a worse move:
27.♕h4? ♗g6 28.♘e6? (28.♘xd6!
♗xd6 29.♗xg6 ♖xg6 30.♘xh7 ♕xh7
31.♕xh7+ ♔xh7 32.♖xg6) 28...♘xe6
29.dxe6 ♕xe6, and the game ended
in a draw after a few moves.
27...♗xd6 28.♕xd6 ♕g7

29.♘f7+
29.♗xf5 ♖xf5 30.♘e6 ♘xe6
31.♕xe6+–
29...♖xf7
29...♕xf7 30.♕e5+ ♖g7 31.♖xg7
**30.♖xg7 ♖fxg7 31.♖xg7 ♖xg7
32.♕f8+ ♖g8 33.♕xf5+–**

126

Solution 72

Bartosz Fiszer 2009
Marc Andria Maurizzi 1947

European Youth Chess Championship
Mamaia 2017 (U10 Open)

41.♖hg7+!
The game continued with 41.♖dg7+?
♔f8 42.♖f7+ ♔g8 43.♖fg7+
(43.♗xe4 dxe4 44.♖fg7+ (44.♖e7 e3
(44...♖d8=) 45.e6 ♖xe6=) 44...♔f8
45.♖d7 ♔g8 46.♖hg7+ ♔f8 47.♖df7+
♔e8 48.♖f4 ♖d8 49.♖g8+ ♔d7
50.♖xd8+ ♔xd8 51.♖xe4 ♖b6±)
43...♔f8 44.♖f7+ ♔g8 ½-½. This
important and interesting game was
played in the penultimate round.
The French boy (Black) won the
championship, while the Polish boy
finished fourth.

41...♔h8
The black king is forced into the
corner, and the white rooks can
prepare the decisive attack; 41...♔f8
42.♖df7+ ♔e8 43.♗b5+–.

42.♗xe4! dxe4 43.♖ge7! e3
43...g5 44.e6 ♖xe6 45.♖xe6+–
44.e6+– e2?! 45.♖h7+ ♔g8
46.♖dg7+ ♔f8 47.e7+ ♔e8 48.♖g8+
♔d7 49.e8+♕ ♔d6 50.♖xg6+
♔d5 51.♖xh5+ ♔d4 52.♖g4+ ♔d3
53.♖d5#

Solution 73

Yaroslav Remizov 2146
Kaan Kucuksari 2319

European Youth Chess Championship
Mamaia 2017 (U14 Open)

25...♕e4+!
Black avoids an unfavourable trade
of queens with this move, while
the game continued with 25...♖hf8?
26.♕d3! ♘e5 (26...♕xd3 27.♖xd3
♔c7 28.♘xd8 ♖xd8 29.♔g2 ♖e8
30.♖d2=) 27.♕xe3 ♖xd1+ 28.♔g2
♘xc4 29.♕xg5 ♖d2+ 30.♔h3 ♖f2=.
Later, White won. The following
day, Remizov finished the
championship with a draw and took
the bronze medal.

26.♔g1
26.♕g2? ♕xc4 27.♘xh8 ♕g8-+
26...♖hf8 27.c3
  A) 27.♗b3 ♕g4 28.♖d2 ♖de8-+;
  B) 27.♕d3? ♘c5! 28.♕xd8+ ♖xd8
29.♖xd8+ ♔c7 30.b3 ♕xc2-+
27...♕e7
And Black is clearly better. For
example:
28.♕f5 ♘b6 29.♖xd8+ ♕xd8
30.♕e5+ ♕c7 31.♕xc7+ ♔xc7
32.♘xg5 ♖e8 33.♗f7 ♖e1+ 34.♔f2
♖b1 35.♗xh5 ♖xb2+ 36.♗e2
♖xa2-+

Solution 74

Ekin Baris Ozenir 2030
Vladislav Larkin 1932

European Youth Chess Championship
Prague 2016 (U12 Open)

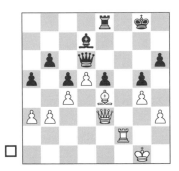

39.h4!
In the game, after 39.♕d3?! ♖f8
40.♗h7+ ♔g7 41.♖xf8 ♔xf8 42.♗f5
♗e8, White was only slightly better.
39...♖f8
39...gxh4?! 40.g5! ♖f8 (40...♗c8 41.g6
♕c7 42.♕xh6 ♕g7 43.♕xh4; 40...
hxg5 41.♕xg5+ ♔h8 42.♕xh4+ ♔g8
43.♕h7#) 41.gxh6 ♖xf2 42.♕g5+
♔f7 43.h7+–
40.♖xf8+ ♕xf8 41.hxg5

With a great advantage for White.
For example: 41...♗xg4 42.gxh6 ♕f6
43.♕g3 ♕g5 44.♗d3 ♕c1 45.♗f1
♕f4 46.♕xf4 exf4 47.♗d3+–

Solution 75

Dmitry Kirillov 2137
Maksim Tsaruk 2060

European Youth Chess Championship
Mamaia 2017 (U12 Open)

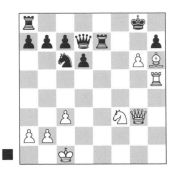

27...♕e6!
The queen works very well on the
sixth rank. Other possibilities:
  A) 27...♕e8?! 28.gxh7+ ♔h8 29.♖g5
♖xh7 30.♗g7+ ♖xg7 31.♖xg7 ♕e3+
32.♔c2 ♕e4+ 33.♔d2 ♕b1 34.♖xc7
♕xb2+ 35.♔d1 ♕b1+ 36.♔d2=;
  B) 27...♖ae8?! 28.♗g5 hxg6 29.♗xe7
♘xe7 30.♖h3, followed by 31.♕h4+,
is unclear;
  C) 27...♘e5?! 28.♘xe5 ♖xe5
29.gxh7+ ♔h8 30.♖xe5 dxe5
31.♕xe5+ ♔xh7 32.♗e3, and White
has sufficient compensation for the
exchange.
28.gxh7+
28.♗g5? ♕xg6–+
28...♔h8 29.♖h1
The players were in time trouble,
and the game continued with
29.♗f4?! (29.♖g5? ♕xh6–+) 29...♖f8?!
(29...♕xa2) 30.♗h6 ♖a8?! (30...♖fe8)
31.♘h4?! (31.♖h1 ♖ae8∓) 31...♕e1+
32.♕xe1 ♖xe1+ 33.♔d2 ♖e6–+.
29...♖ae8∓

Solution 76

Magdalena Pawicka 1826
Veronika Shubenkova 1505

European Youth Chess Championship
Mamaia 2017 (U10 Girls)

37...h5!

The game continued with 37...
b5? 38.♗e3±. Black was able to
hold the game and later won the
championship.
38.♕h4 ♘f5! 39.♕xh5 ♕xg2+!
40.♔xg2 ♘xf4+–+

Solution 77

Vincent Tsay 2033
Volodar Murzin 1643

World Cadets Chess Championship
Poços de Caldas 2017 (U12 Open)

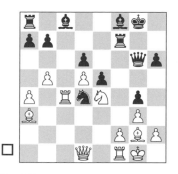

24.♘xd6!

The game went 24.♖xd4? exd4
25.♕xd4 ♗f5, and Black was better
and eventually won. Tsay (USA)

recovered from this loss and won
the championship with 8.5/11 on
tiebreak over Sindarov (Uzbekistan)
and Murzin (Russia).
24.♗xd6!? ♗g7 25.♗b4±
24...♖d7
24...♗xd6 25.♗xd6 ♕xd6?!

analysis diagram

26.♖xc8+! ♖xc8 27.♕xg4+ ♔h8
28.♕xc8++–
25.♘xc8 ♗xa3 26.♖e1 ♕g7 27.♖xd4
exd4 28.♖e8+ ♗f8 29.♘e7+ ♖xe7
30.♖xa8+–

Solution 78

Wadhawan Daaevik 1561
Abhimanyu Mishra 1774

World Cadets Chess Championship
Poços de Caldas 2017 (U8 Open)

55.♕e2!

The game continued with 55.♗c1?
♕c2 56.♕d2?! ♕xd2 57.♗xd2

♘d5–+. Black won the game and later took the silver medal.

55...♘d5

55...♔g6 56.g4 ♘d5 57.gxf5+ ♔xf5 58.♕g4+ ♔e5 59.♕g3+ ♔f5 60.♕g4+ ♔e5=

56.♕h5 ♕xd2 57.♕f7+ ♔h8 58.♕f8+ ♔h7=

Solution 79
Ilya Makoveev   1942
Aydin Suleymanli   1910
European Youth Chess Championship
Porec 2015 (U10 Open)

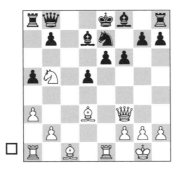

15.♖xe6!

The game continued with 15.♗e3?, and Black, instead of playing 15...♗xb5 (or 15...♘g6) 16.♗xb5+ ♔f7, with unclear play, preferred 15...♔f7? 16.♗f4+–.

15...♗xe6

15...♔f7 16.♗f4 ♕d8 17.♖xf6+ gxf6 18.♗c7+–

16.♗f4 ♕d8 17.♗c7! ♕d7 18.♘d6+ ♕xd6 19.♗xd6+–

Makoveev won the gold.

Solution 80
Annapoorni Meiyappan   1658
Deshmukh Divya   1993
World Cadets Chess Championship
Poços de Caldas 2017 (U12 Girls)

36.♖a6+!

The game continued with 36.h3?? (36.♖f1? ♖xc7 37.♖xf6+ ♔e7 38.♖xc7+ ♔xf6 39.♖xh7 ♘e5∓) 36...♖xc7–+.

36...♔d7 37.♖xf6

The rook attacks and defends.

37...♖c8

37...♖c1+ 38.♖f1 ♖xf1+ 39.♔xf1+–

38.♖b8 ♖a5 39.♖f7+ ♔c6 40.♖xc8 ♖a1+ 41.♖f1 ♖xa7 42.h3 ♖c7 43.♖xc7+ ♔xc7 44.♖f7+

And White has a great advantage.

Solution 81

Ningxuan Wang

Abhimanyu Mishra 1774

World Cadets Chess Championship

Poços de Caldas 2017 (U8 Open)

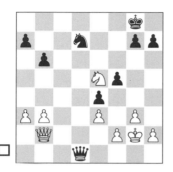

31.♕c3!

A finesse. The game went 31.b4?!
♕d5 32.♘xd7 ♕xd7=.

31...♘xe5

31...♕d5 32.♕c8+ ♘f8 33.♕xf5
♕xb3 34.♕xe4

**32.♕c8+ ♔f7 33.♕xf5+ ♔g8
34.♕e6+ ♔f8 35.♕xe5 ♕xb3
36.♕b8+ ♔f7 37.♕xa7+ ♔f6 38.♕c7**
White is a pawn up, although Black
retains good drawing chances.

Solution 82

Xiaoxi Wei 1453

A R Ilamparthi 1492

World Cadets Chess Championship

Poços de Caldas 2017 (U8 Open)

40.♗xf3!

A) 40.♖xf8? ♖xf8 41.♕h3 ♕d4+
42.♔e1 ♕a1+ 43.♔f2 ♕d4+=;

B) 40.♖h6+? ♔e7 41.♖e6+ ♔d8
42.♖d6+ ♔e7=;

C) The game went 40.♖xf7+? ♖xf7
41.♔g3 ♕f4+ 42.♔h3 ♔g7 43.♖h5 f2
44.d6 ♕e3+ 45.♔g2 ♕e4+ 46.♔g3
♕f4+ 47.♔h3 ♕d2 48.d7 ♕e3+
49.♔g2 ♕e4+ 50.♔g3 ♕f4+ 51.♔h3
♖f8 52.♗e2 ½-½.

40...♕f5

40...♔e7 41.♔g2 ♕c2+ 42.♔e2

**41.♖xf7+ ♖xf7 42.♕h3 ♕xh3
43.♖xh3+−**

Solution 83

Svitlana Demchenko 1985

Elizaveta Solozhenkina 2248

World Youth Chess Championship

Montevideo 2017 (U14 Girls)

We saw this game a few moves
earlier, in the part on strategy.
Black didn't play accurately, and
now White had a nice combination
that didn't appear on the board.

30.cxb5?

A) Not 30.♘f5? ♘xd3 31.♕g5 ♘h5
32.♘h6+ ♔h8 33.♘xf7+ ♔g8 34.c5!?
dxc5 35.d6 ♘xf2 36.♘h6+ ♔h8
37.♘f7+ ♔g8=.

B) 30.c5! dxc5 31.♖xf6! gxf6
32.♕h6 cxb4+ (32...c4+ 33.♔h1!?

131

♘xd3 34.♘h5 ♘f2+ 35.♔h2+−)
33.♔h2 ♕d6 (33...♕c7 34.♕xh7+
♔f8 35.♕h8+ ♔e7 36.♕xf6+ ♔f8
37.d6+−) 34.♗xh7+ (34.♔h1?? ♘xd3)
34...♖h8 35.♗e4+ ♔g8 36.♖xf6
♘f3+ 37.gxf3 ♖c2+ 38.♗xc2 ♖e2+
39.♔h1 ♖e1+ 40.♔g2 ♖g1+ 41.♔xg1
♕xg3+ 42.♔f1+−

30...axb5

30...♘xd3 31.♕xd3 ♖e3 32.♕f5 ♖f8
33.♕g5 h6 34.♕h4 ♖xg3 35.♕xg3
♘e4 36.♕f4 ♘xf2 37.♖xf2 axb5=

**31.♔h1 ♘xd3 32.♕xd3 ♖e3 33.♕f5
♖f8**

With a roughly even game. The
game ended in a draw.

In the championship, Solozhenkina
(Russia) took bronze, while
Demchenko (Canada) finished in
sixth place.

Solution 84
Guadalupe Milagros Mayeregger 1585
Miruna-Daria Lehaci 1914
World Youth Chess Championship
Montevideo 2017 (U14 Girls)

18...♗e3+!
The right move, controlling the
f2-square. The alternatives:
   A) 18...g6?! 19.♕f2! ♗e7 20.♗xe7
♕xe7 21.♖ae1 ♕d6 22.♕e3 ♔g7
23.♕e7 ♕xe7 24.♖xe7 ♖ad8=;

   B) 18...♘f6?! 19.♗xf8 ♕xf8
20.♘f3 ♗e3+ 21.♔h1 ♘c8 22.♕e5
♘g4 23.♕xd5 ♗e6 24.♕h5 ♘f6
(24...♘f2+ 25.♖xf2 ♗xf2 26.♘e4
♗e3 27.d5±) 25.♕b5, and Black has
insufficient compensation for the
exchange;
   C) 18...♗e7?, the move played
in the game. Now, White played
19.♗b2?, instead of 19.♗xe7 ♕xe7
20.♖ae1 ♕d8 (20...♕d6? 21.♕g4
♖fe8 (21...♘f6 22.♕xg7++−) 22.♘h5
g6 23.♕xd7+−) 21.♘h5, with a
dangerous initiative, for example:
21...♖c8 22.♕g4 ♕g5 23.♕xd7 ♗c6
24.♕f5 ♕xd2 25.♖e7 ♕g5 26.♕xg5
hxg5 27.♖f5±

19.♖f2
19.♔h1 g6 20.♕g4 ♗xd2 21.♘h5 ♗g5
22.♗xf8 ♘xf8−+

**19...g6 20.♕f3 ♗xd4 21.♗xf8 ♕xf8
22.♖e1 ♘e5 23.♖xe5 ♗xe5−+**

Solution 85
Valentin Mitev 2056
Noah Fecker 2166
World Youth Chess Championship
Montevideo 2017 (U14 Open)

16...♘xd5!
16...♘c5 is interesting, but seems
less promising after 17.♘c6 ♔f8
18.♖he1 ♖xa4 19.♖xa4 ♕xa4
20.♕xa4 ♘xa4 21.♗c3 ♘xc3 22.bxc3.

17.exd5 ♗xd4 18.♘xd4 ♕xd5+ 19.♘f3
19.f3 ♕xd4 20.♖he1 e6∓
19...♘e5 20.♕d1
20.♖a3 c3! 21.♕d1 cxd2 22.♕xd2
♕xd2 23.♘xd2 ♖c2 24.♘f3 ♘c4∓
20...♘xf3 21.♕xf3 ♕xd2 22.♖b7
♖ca8 23.♖hd1 ♕g5 24.h4 ♕f6∓
And Black won.

Solution 86
Saina Salonika 2022
Nazerke Nurgali 2068
World Youth Chess Championship
Montevideo 2017 (U14 Girls)

19...♘xg2?
19...♗xh3! 20.♖e3 ♖xe3 21.♕xe3 ♗f5
22.♕g3 ♘g6 23.♗c1 ♖xd4, and Black
is winning.
20.♘xf6+!
  A) Not 20.♔xg2? ♗xh3+ 21.♔h2
♗xf1–+;
  B) Interesting is the computer
move 20.♖e5!?. For example:
20...♘h4! (20...fxe5? 21.♕g5 ♘f4
22.♘f6+ ♔h8 23.♗xg7+ ♗xg7
24.♕h4+ ♘h5 25.♕xh5+ ♗h6
26.♕xh6+#) 21.♘xf6+ gxf6 22.♖h7+
♔xh7 23.♗xf8 ♘f3+ 24.♔h1 ♘g5
25.♖xg5 fxg5 26.♕xg5 ♗d5+ 27.♔g1
♖xf8 28.♕h5+ ♔g7 29.♕g5+=
20...gxf6 21.♗xf8 ♔xf8 22.♔xg2
♗xh3+
And we arrive to the next puzzle.

Solution 87
Saina Salonika 2022
Nazerke Nurgali 2068
World Youth Chess Championship
Montevideo 2017 (U14 Girls)

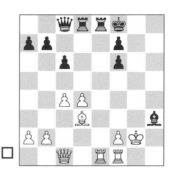

23.♔h1?
23.♔h2! ♗e6 (23...♗g2? 24.♕h6+)
24.♕f4 ♔e7 25.♔g2 ♕d7 26.♖e4
♖h8 27.♖fe1 ♖dg8+ 28.♔f3, with
chances for both sides.
23...♗g2+! 24.♔xg2 ♕g4+ 25.♔h2
25.♔h1 ♔g7 26.♖xe8 ♖xe8 27.♕c2
♖h8+ 28.♗h7 f5–+
25...♔g7 0-1

Solution 88
Martha Samadashvili 1995
Miruna-Daria Lehaci 1914
World Youth Chess Championship
Montevideo 2017 (U14 Girls)

27...♖h6!

If Black is able to exchange the most active white piece, the bishop pair will become very dangerous. Moves such as 27...f6 28.e6 fxg5 29.♖c8+ ♗d8 30.♗xg5 0-0 31.♖xd8 ♖xd8 32.♗xd8 ♗xe6 or 27...♗d8 28.♖c5 ♗a2 29.d5 ♗xg5 30.♗xg5 ♔d7 lead to an equal ending, while the move played in the game, 27...♔d8?, could have been punished by 28.♖xb7! (the game continued with 28.♖c1? ♔d7 29.♘f3 ♖c8∓, and Black won) 28...♗xb7 29.♘xf7+ ♔d7 30.♘xh8 ♗a3! 31.♗c3 ♗c1, where Black is slightly worse.

28.♖c8+

28.♘f3 ♖c6 29.♖xb7 (29.♖xc6 ♗xc6 30.♘e1 ♗d8 31.♘d3 b6 32.axb6 ♗xb6∓) 29...♖c2 30.♖b8+ ♔d7 31.♗e3 ♖a2 32.♔h2 (32.♖g8 g6 33.♖g7 f4 34.♗xf4 ♖xf2 35.♗e3 ♖e2 36.♗g5 ♗xg5 37.♘xg5 ♔e7–+) 32...♖xa5, and Black is better and has a dangerous passed pawn.

28...♔d7 29.♖b8 ♖g6 30.♘f3 ♗d8 31.♘e1 b5 32.axb6 ♗xb6∓

Solution 89

Shoham Cohen Revivo 2188
Kazybek Nogerbek 2358

World Youth Chess Championship
Montevideo 2017 (U14 Open)

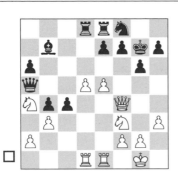

22.bxc4!

The alternatives are less promising:

A) 22.e6?! f6 23.d6 g5 24.♕xc4 (24.♕g4 ♖xd6 25.♖xd6 exd6 is unclear, for example: 26.♘d4 ♗c8 27.♘b2 cxb3 28.♘c4 ♕c5 29.axb3 ♔h8 30.h4 ♘xe6 31.♘xe6 ♕d5 32.♕h5 ♖xe6=) 24...♗xf3 25.d7 (25.gxf3 ♖xd6 26.♖xd6 exd6 27.♕c6 ♕d8 28.♘b6 ♖xe6 29.♕b7+ ♔g8=) 25...♗xd1 26.♖xd1 ♕e5 27.♕xb4 (27.dxe8+♘ ♖xe8 28.♕xb4 ♘xe6) 27...♘xe6 28.♖e1 ♕d5 29.♘b6 ♕c6 30.dxe8♕ ♖xe8, and White has only a minimal advantage;

B) 22.♘g5?! ♗xd5 23.♖xd5 ♕xd5 24.♘b6 ♕c6 25.♕xf7+ ♔h8 26.♘xc4 h6 27.♘e4 ♕e6 28.♕f3 ♘d7, with mutual chances.

22...♕xa4 23.♘g5 f6?!

Better was 23...h6 24.♘xf7 g5 25.♕f3, and White has a dangerous initiative. For example: 25...♘g6 (25...♖c8 26.h4! ♖xc4 27.hxg5 ♕c2 (27...♘g6 28.gxh6+ ♔h7 29.♘g5+ ♔xh6 30.♕e3 ♘f4 31.♘h3 ♕a3 32.♕b6+ e6 33.♘xf4 ♖xf4 34.♕xb7+–) 28.gxh6+ ♔h7 29.♖c1! ♕xc1 30.♖xc1 ♖xc1+ 31.♔h2 ♘g6 32.♘g5+ ♔xh6 33.♘e6 ♖c4 34.g4+–) 26.♘xd8 ♖xd8 27.e6 ♖f8 28.♕e3 ♔h7 29.♖d2±

24.♘e4 ♘d7

25.exf6+

The game went 25.e6?! ♘e5 26.♘c5 ♕xa2 (26...♕c2!?) 27.♖xe5?

(27.♘xb7±) 27...fxe5 28.♕xe5+ ♔g8
29.♘xb7 ♖b8, with advantage to
Black. The game ended in a draw.

25...exf6

25...♘xf6 26.♘c5 ♕c2 27.♘xb7 e5
28.♕e3+−

26.♕c7

26...♔g8

26...♖xe4 27.♕xd8 ♖xe1+ 28.♖xe1
♔h6 29.♕c7 ♗a8 30.♖e7+−

27.♘d6 ♖f8 28.♕xb7+−

Solution 90

Mieszko Mis — 2245
Abilmansur Abdilkhair — 1968

World Youth Chess Championship
Montevideo 2017 (U14 Open)

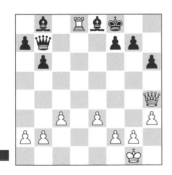

This time, you had to find the only
defence.

31...♗e5!

A) 31...a5? is insufficient: 32.♕a4
b5 33.♕a3+ b4 34.♕a4

analysis diagram

34...♗h2+ (34...♕e7 35.♖xb8+−)
35.♔h1 ♕e7 36.♖xe8+ ♕xe8
37.♕xe8+ ♔xe8 38.♔xh2, and
White wins the ending easily;

   B) The game continued 31...♗c7?
32.♕b4+ 1-0.

32.♕a4

32.♕b4+ ♕e7 33.♖a8 ♕xb4 34.cxb4
♗xb2 35.♖xa7 b5=

32...♕e7 33.♖a8

33...♕e6!?

An active choice. Possible is 33...a5
34.♕c6 ♕e6 35.♕xe6 fxe6 36.♖a6
♗c7, where White is a little better,
but Black should draw with precise
play.

After 33...♕e6!?, play could continue
with

**34.♕xa7 ♕d5 35.♕a4 b5 36.c4
♕xc4 37.♕xc4 bxc4 38.♖c8 ♗xb2
39.a4 ♗c3! 40.♖xc4 ♗a5 41.♖c8
♔e7 42.♖a8 ♗c7 43.a5 ♗c6 44.♖g8
♗xa5 45.♖xg7 ♔f6=**

Afterword

Here, I wish to sum up the main suggestions I gave you in this book.

Firstly, repeat the exercises a few times.

Secondly, practise the following tools:
- Prophylactic thinking;
- Blunder checking;
- Calculation technique and combinative vision;
- Good time management.

Good luck!

Franco Zaninotto

Index of players (numbers refer to pages)

Read by club players in 116 countries!

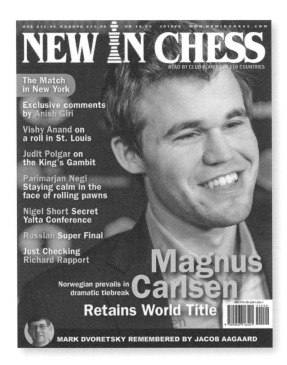

New In Chess magazine has regular contributions from all the world's best players: Carlsen, Kramnik, Aronian, Anand, Nakamura, Caruana, Grischuk many others. Subscribers get more than 800 pages per year of news, views and training, with regular columns by Judit Polgar, Nigel Short,

Matthew Sadler, Parimarjan Negi, honorary editor Jan Timman and contributing editor Anish Giri. You can now download the digital edition on your tablet or smartphone and replay the moves on the interactive chess viewer. Join subscribers from 116 countries and take out an introductory offer today!

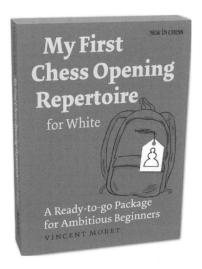
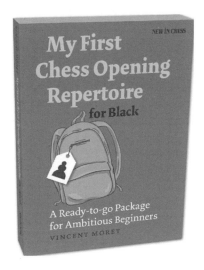

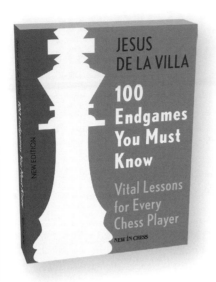

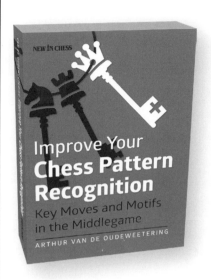